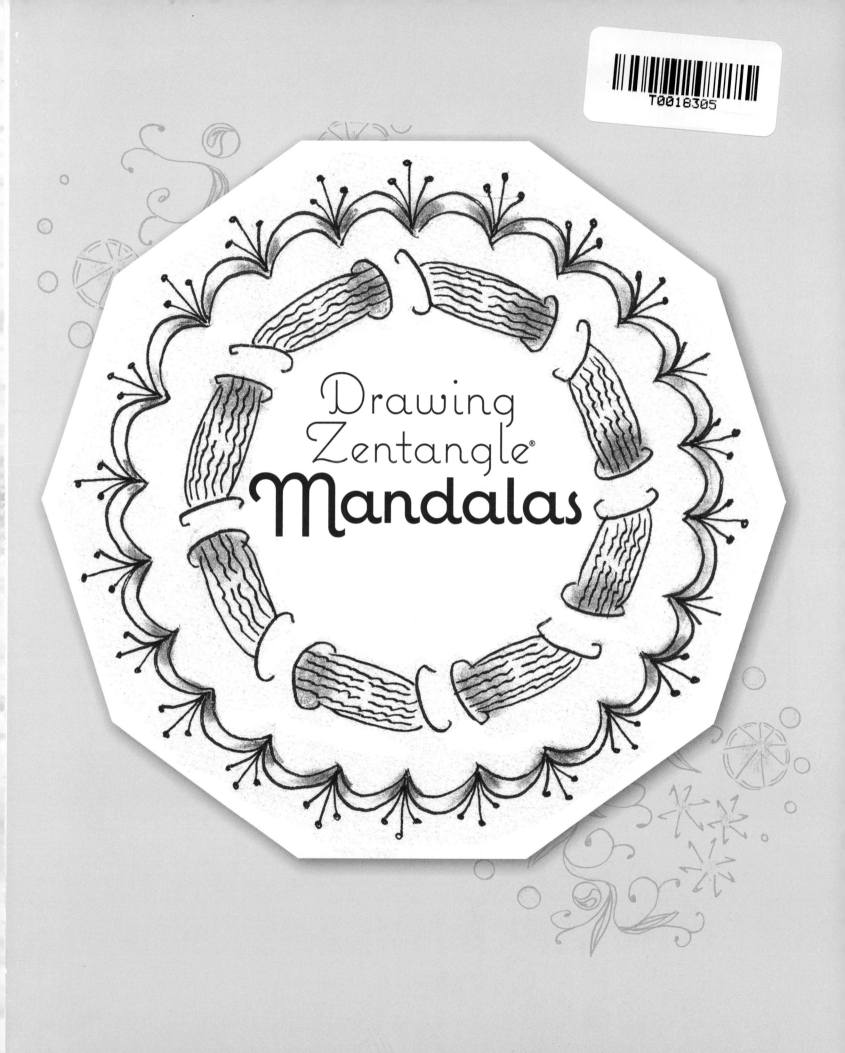

Drawing Zentangle® Mandalas

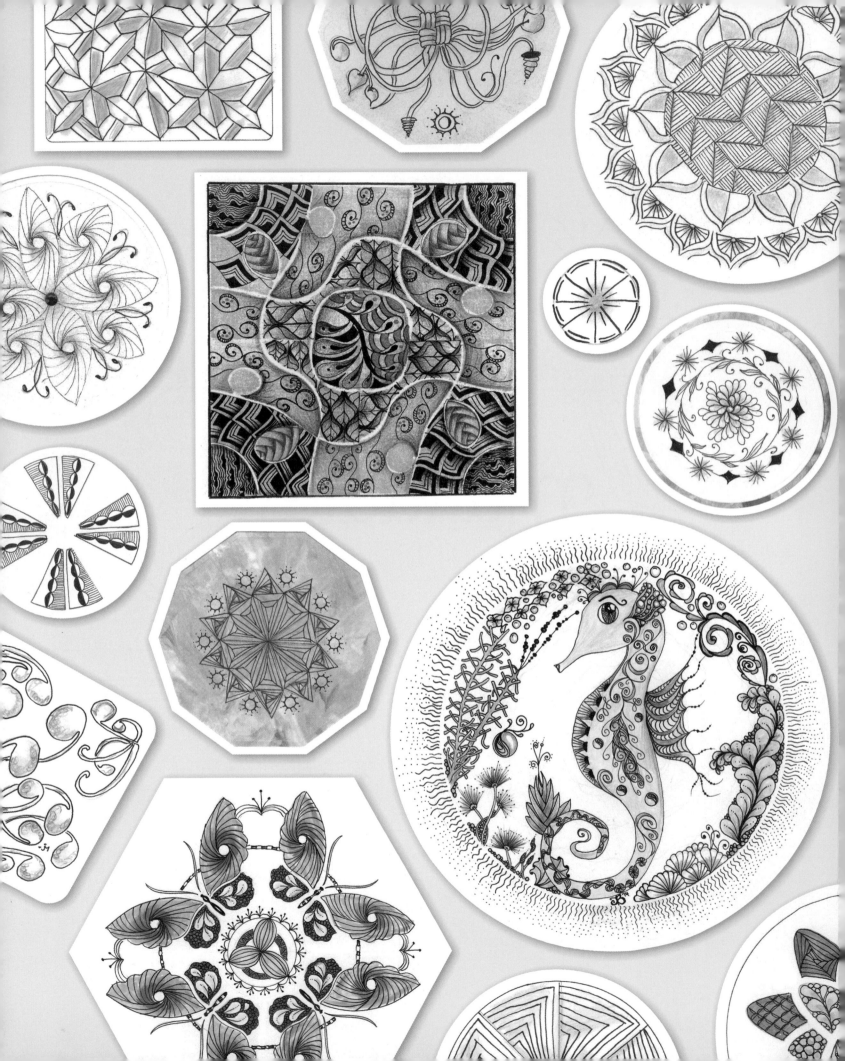

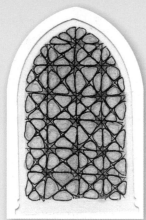
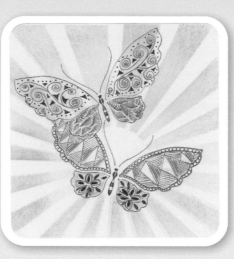

Drawing
Zentangle®
Mandalas

The mindful way to creativity

Jane Marbaix

★
SIRIUS

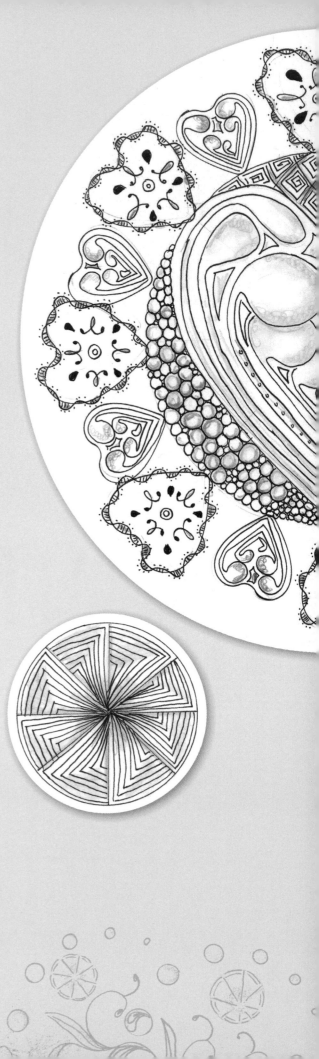

Acknowledgment:
My thanks to the many CZTs worldwide and friends who contributed to this book.

Dreamweaver stencils are available from www.woodware.co.uk and www.
stampendous.com

SIRIUS

This edition published in 2023 by Sirius Publishing, a division of
Arcturus Publishing Limited,
26/27 Bickels Yard, 151–153 Bermondsey Street,
London SE1 3HA

ISBN: 978-1-3988-2620-5
AD004568UK

Printed in China

Contents

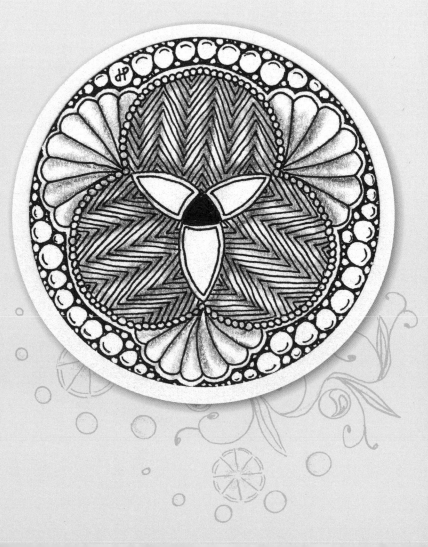

The philosophy of Zentangle

The Zentangle mantra is 'Anything is possible, one stroke at a time' – a philosophy that both inspires confidence and instils a sense of calm. This form of art is one that can be practised successfully by everyone, for even if you think you have no drawing skills you will soon discover that you can achieve lovely results. One of the keys to Zentangle art is always to relax and take your time; the focus is on the present moment, never on the result. It is all about the journey, not the destination.

The Zentangle method was created by Maria Thomas, a talented lettering and botanical artist, and Rick Roberts, the zen of the partnership, having lived as a monk for a period of his life. Rick noticed that while Maria was working she was in a very calm, focused state, so they set about breaking down the patterns they created in an easy-to-follow format so that anyone could create beautiful images by repeating the patterns, known as tangles. Thus, the Zentangle method was born.

Zentangle art is created on a tile which is 9 cm (3½ in) square. The official Zentangle tile is created from Fabriano Tiepolo paper (available from good art shops and online), but some tanglers just use good-quality card stock. In fact, you can tangle on anything, but good materials make all the difference. An artwork bigger than 9 cm (3½ in) square is categorized as Zentangle Inspired Art (ZIA).

You can begin making tangles with just a soft pencil, an 01 (0.25 mm) black pen (my preference is for Sakura Pigma Micron) and a blending stump, also known as a tortillon. An 08 (0.50 mm) pen or Pigma Graphic 1 is ideal for darker areas. I also use stencils and rubber stamps, and for this book a compass and protractor are handy. A good starting point is the kit available from www.zentangle.com.

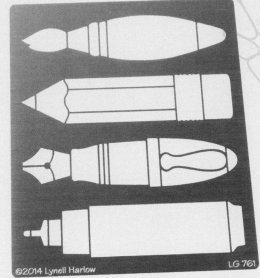

©2014 Lynell Harlow   LG 761

Dreamweaver metal stencils come in a wide range of amazing designs (example left), created by Lynell Harlow. Her husband, Wayne, has done the most beautiful work transforming them (below).

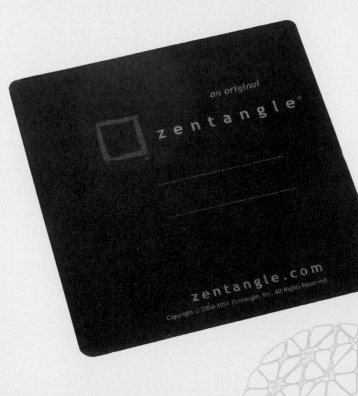

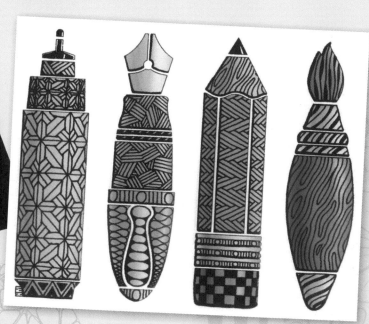

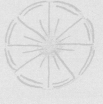

A protractor (above) is a useful tool for creating mandalas. The inner circle of the Zendala below was made with the help of one.

What is a mandala?

The word 'mandala' is Sanskrit and can be loosely translated as 'circle'. A mandala is regarded as a sacred circle representing wholeness. There are plenty of books on mandalas if you want to study the subject in depth; the aim of this book is to introduce the Zentangle equivalent of the mandala, which is called a Zendala. A true mandala is divided into sections, with the same pattern repeated in each section, and while a Zendala may be formed that way it need have no boundaries or set form. Just drawing a string within the circle and filling each space with a pattern will produce something you can admire, making this a fun and easy way to create a Zendala.

Zentangle is a mindful way of self-expression that lends itself to the creation of imagery that aids meditation or at the very least puts the maker into a very calm state of mind. Tangling enables us to create a safe and joyful inner space even when real life may be confronting us with challenges that we are having difficulty coping with. It does not matter if you are not interested in the spiritual side of mandalas or, indeed, creating true mandalas – making a circular design is a enjoyable way to create an artwork that is pleasing to the eye. It is easy to rotate a circle while you work on it, too.

Getting started with tangles

In the Zentangle method, tangles (patterns) are broken down into simple steps so that it is easy to re-create each tangle. Each tile (or square piece of card) is divided into spaces by 'strings' and each space will have a different tangle in it. There are many tangles to choose from. In the tiles below, Crescent Moon, Tortuca, Poke Root and Tipple are used, all of them original Zentangle patterns created by Rick Roberts and Maria Thomas or their daughter, Molly Hollibaugh.

Tile No. 1 with Z string

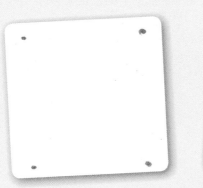

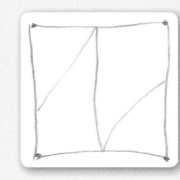

Draw a pencil line, known as a string, to create spaces within the tile. Here we shall draw a string in the shape of a Z.

Using your pencil, draw a dot in each corner of the tile.

Join up the dots lightly with your pencil to form a border (this line does not need to be straight).

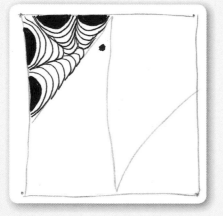
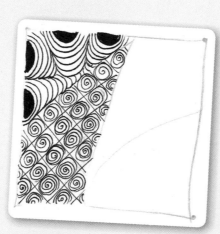
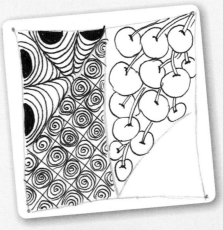

Then draw Poke Root.

Now take your pen (Sakura Pigma Micron 01 black), choose a tangle and fill one of the spaces you have created. The first tangle used here is Crescent Moon, put in the top left-hand corner space.

Next, draw Tortuca.

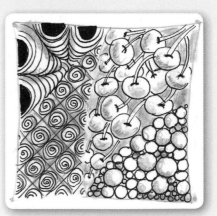

Lastly, draw Tipple in the remaining space, making different-sized circles for a pleasing effect. Now shade the completed tile with your pencil.

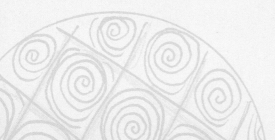

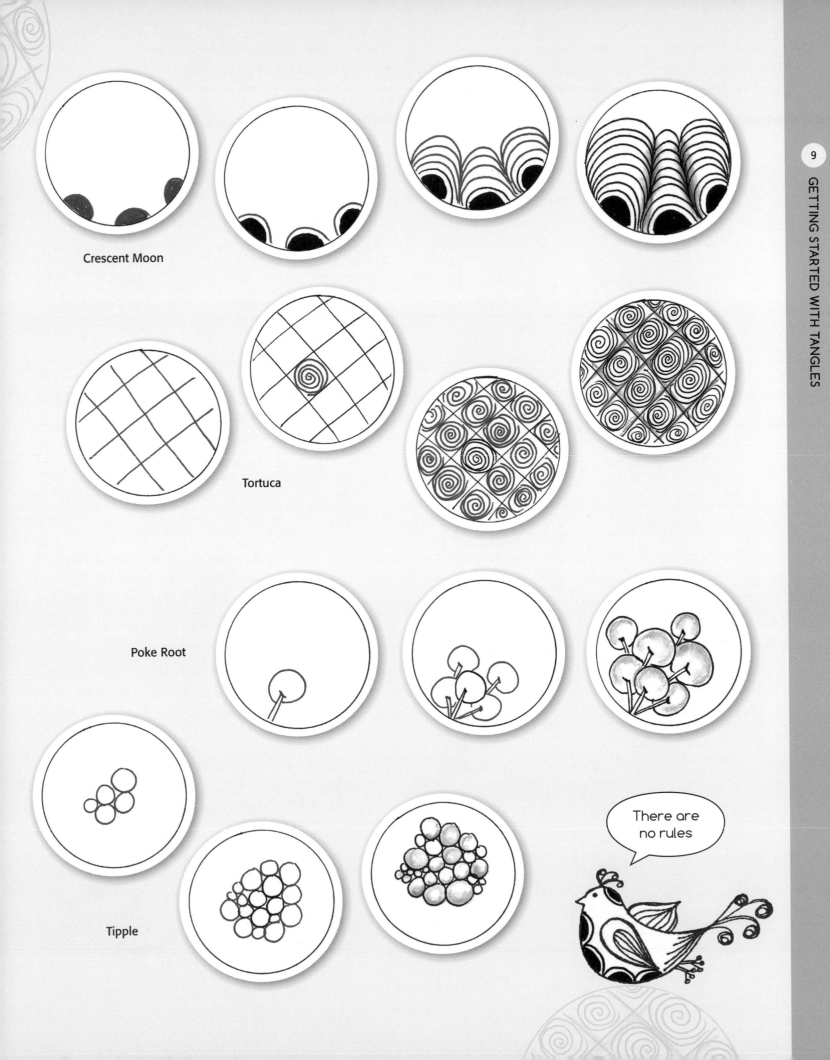

Crescent Moon

Tortuca

Poke Root

Tipple

There are no rules

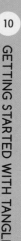

Tile No. 2 with triangle string

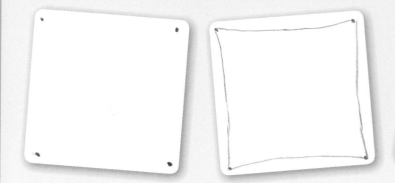

Start this string the same way as the first one, by making a dot in each corner and drawing a line between the dots. This string is in the shape of a triangle – it doesn't need to be a uniform shape. This will give you four spaces for your tangles.

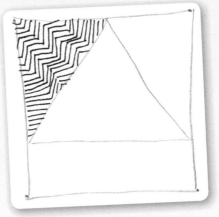

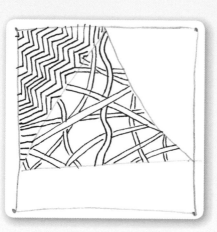

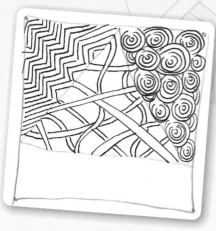

In the first space draw Static, which looks simple but can be greatly enhanced with shading to give it a three-dimensional look. In the final step opposite I have used two different types of shading.

The next space will be the central triangle, filled in with Hollibaugh. You can make the lines straight or wavy, thick or thin.

Next is Printemps in the top right-hand corner. Go slowly with this tangle, leaving a small gap in the lines to create a highlight.

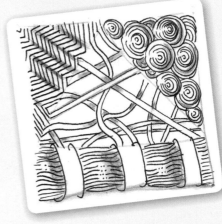

The tangle at the bottom of the tile is Zander. Create highlights by leaving some gaps between the lines, with two or three dots in the gap. Finally, shade the tangles.

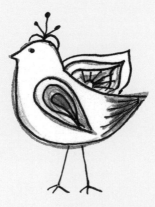

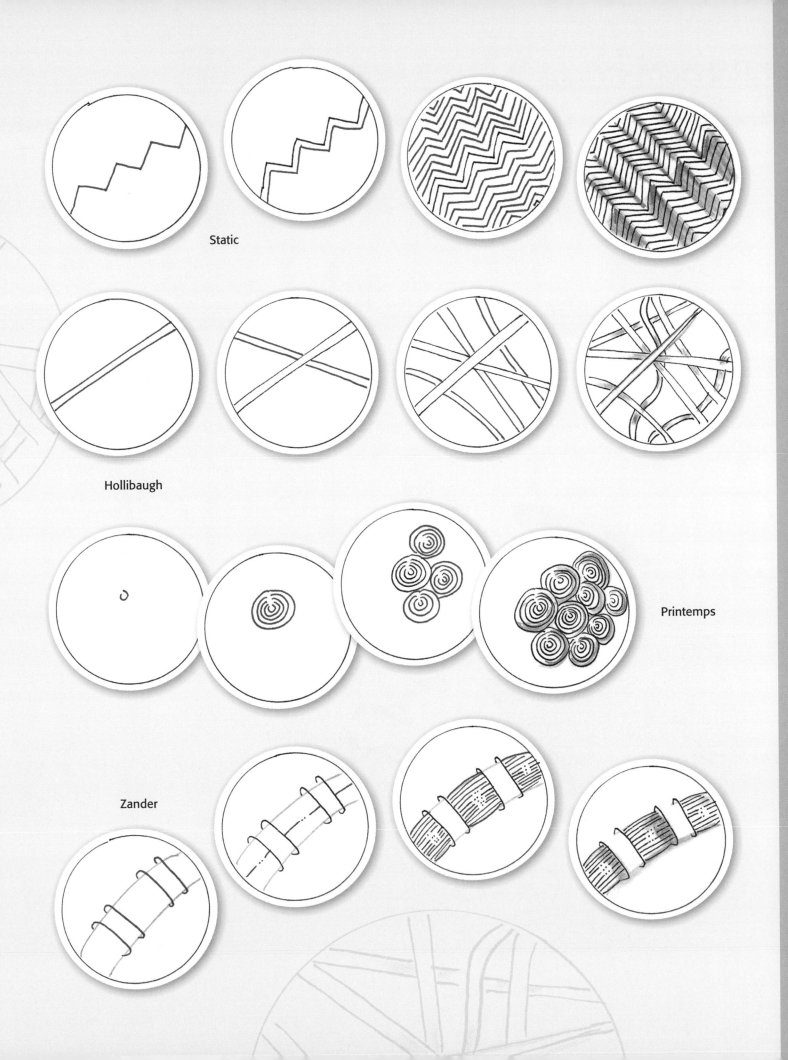

Static

Hollibaugh

Printemps

Zander

Random strings

Using a circular protractor, make a circle and then draw some random strings – just go with the flow and then fill in with tangles. Strings are only guidelines and you don't need to keep strictly within their borders. I have used Crescent Moon, Poke Root, Static, Zander, Tipple, Hollibaugh and Tortuca.

Making a Zendala

The next step is a Zendala with a random string. There is no set pattern to this – just draw a circle with your circular protractor and then use it to draw semi-circles anywhere and any which way within the outer circle.

The tangles used here are Crescent Moon, N'Zeppel, Florz (variation), Flux, Meer, Onamato, Poke Leaf, Hollibaugh filled in with a bit of Tipple and black background, Poke Root and Paradox. It is surprising just how many tangles you can fit in one circle.

Using a compass

This is one of the simplest forms to make with a compass. Draw a circle, then make a point on the circle and draw a part circle going through the centre. Next, place the point of the compass at the end of the circle you have drawn and draw another part circle. Continue in this way all round the circle until you have formed a flower shape. The 'petals' can be filled in with tangles or you can leave them blank and fill in the background. The top circle has Tipple and N'Zeppel; below, I have used Fassett in the background and Marbaix on the petals.

45-degree mandala

To create a true mandala, use a compass to draw the outer size you would like. Mark points on the circumference at each 45 degrees and then draw lines through the circle to divide the mandala into eight equal parts. Here I used my protractor to draw some semi-circles between the spaces and add a circle in the middle.

I started in the centre, which is where one often starts drawing a mandala. I used the tangle Maryfield, then added another line beside the ones I had already drawn and drew these lines in pen. I added some small circles for effect and then used the tangle Betweed in between the lines and a variation of Marbaix in the semi-circles around the edge.

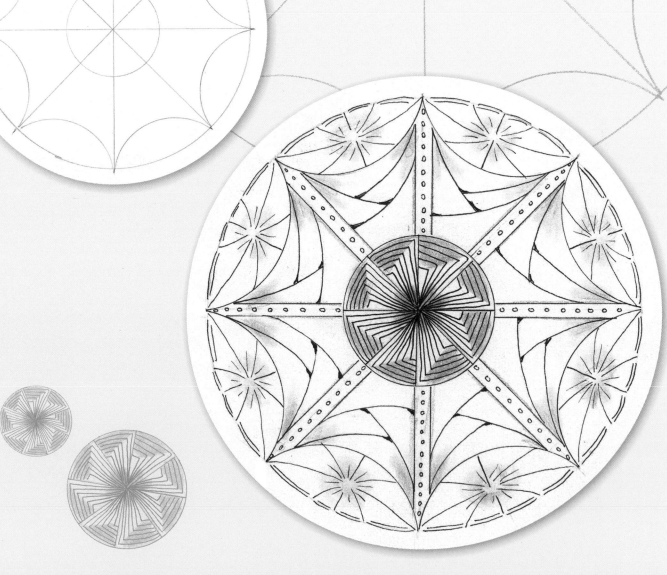

Shading

Adding some shading will transform your tangles and add to the meditative, relaxing process of creating artwork. Use either a soft black pencil, such as a 2B, or some coloured pencils – the Koh-i-Noor Magic Pencil is my own favourite. I have shown some basic shading ideas for you to practise with, learning how to make smooth, even tone or a more textured effect.

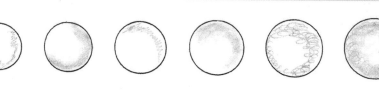

Circles

A circle can be partially shaded towards the edge or all around, giving a more solid appearance.

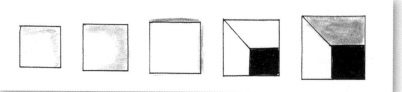

Squares

I have shaded both inside the square and outside for a different effect. In the fourth and fifth squares the tangle Cubine contributes to a three-dimensional illusion.

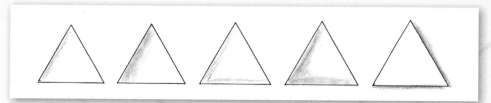

Triangles

With a triangle you have a choice of three sides to shade on the inner or outer edge.

Hollibaugh

This small example of Hollibaugh has shading where one band overlays another; you can see how three-dimensional it looks compared to the one that lacks shading.

Static

You can considerably alter the appearance of a zigzag tangle such as Static by shading different parts of the lines.

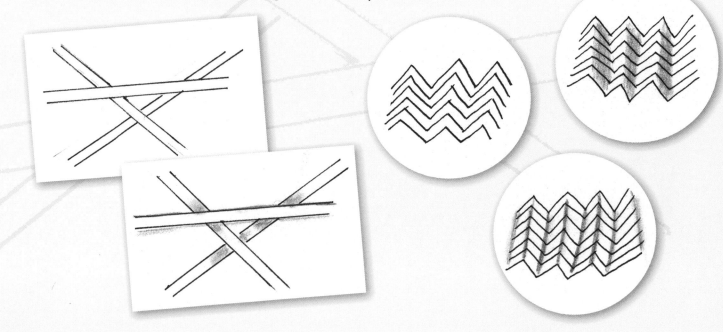

Shaded Zendala

This Zendala starts with a circle and is then divided into four by means of straight lines through the middle. I formed triangles randomly around the lines, which gives a very angular finish.

The tangles used are Cubine, Paradox, Crescent Moon, Fassett, Emingle, Marbaix, Howda, Cruze with Luv-a, Tipple, LaCePa, single Fassett, Bales, N'Zeppel, Static, LogJam and Hollibaugh.

Triple Zendala

On this page I have drawn three overlapping circles, using a compass, to make a triple Zendala. Experiment to see what pleasing structures you can come up with using overlapping forms.

For my first circle I used a KalaDalas stencil (see p.44) and filled it in with Paradox and Flux; the next one has a random string with Poke Root, N'Zeppel, Florz, Cadent and Onamato. The lower Zendala again has a random string and is filled in with Bales, W2, Crescent Moon, Zander, Tipple and Knightsbridge.

Traditional mandala

This was made by using a compass to divide a circle into eight, marking the points at 45 degrees on a protractor. I started by drawing Flux on each line. I then drew triangles around the edge with Paradox inside and from there I drew a straight line down the middle, colouring one side and drawing straight lines across the other. It is the colouring that adds depth to this simple mandala. I used a Copic marker for the colour, which gives a very even finish, as does a Promarker.

Heart mandala

I have a hearts template that I used for this mandala. I used three different sizes of hearts. In the centre heart I used Mooka with Emingle and Tipple in the circle behind; the small hearts are alternately Mooka and Oolo. The Oolo hearts have Organza around the edge.

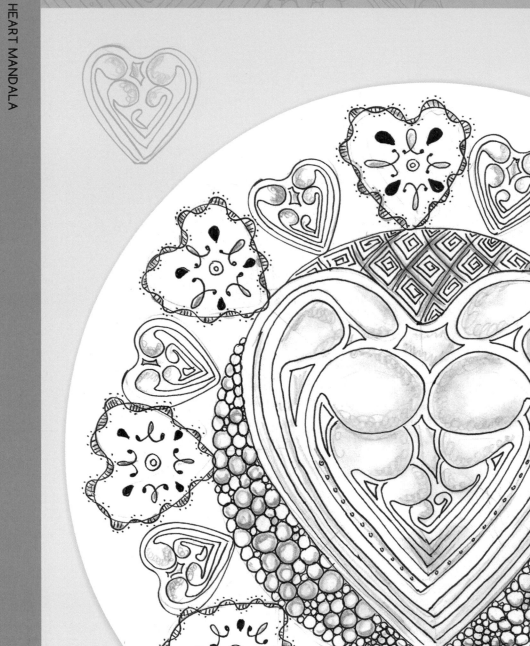

Using multiple circles

For this artwork I used a compass to draw two semi-circles and then joined them up with two more. I then drew a circle in the centre and four more circles around the outside. This design could be done in many different ways if you experiment with your larger outline circles.

In the centre, Marbaix and Crescent Moon are used, with Btl Joos for the circle lines. The top circle is Flux with Tipple. On the right are Florz, N'Zeppel, Tipple and Flux variation. On the left, Static and Flux are used with Tipple; bottom, Marbaix, Knightsbridge and Btl Joos.

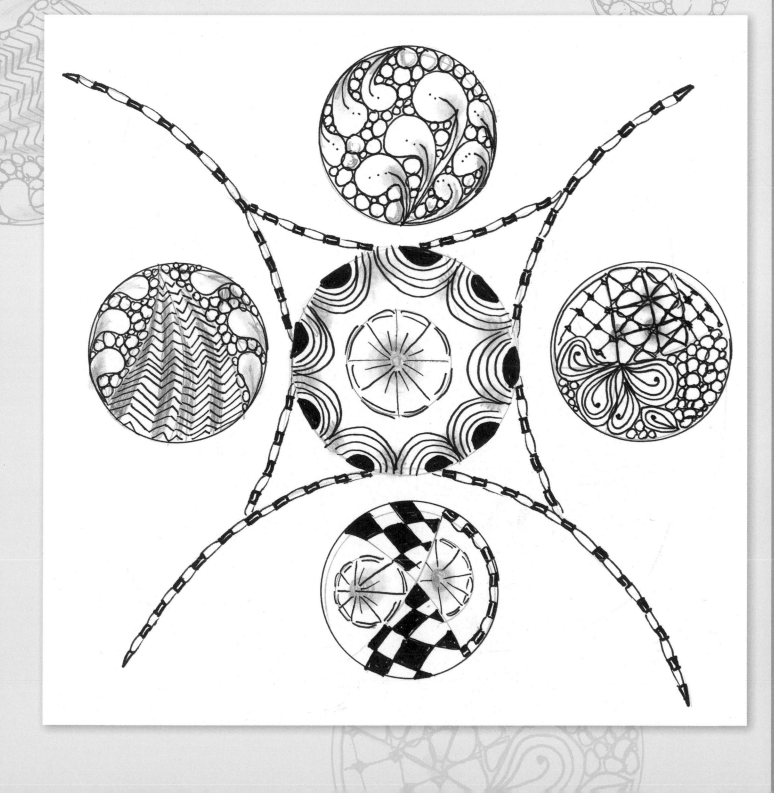

Zentangle friends: Dr Lesley Roberts

The three beautiful Zendalas here and overleaf are by Dr Lesley Roberts, and as you can see a lot of time has gone into creating them. They are all Mooka. Lesley has become a real expert on this tangle and she explains it in depth in her Mooka step-outs.

I have spent many happy hours drawing different forms of Mooka, 'infurled' and 'unfurled'. The more I practise it, the more I continue to love it – it is definitely not a tangle that is easy to get the hang of at the first attempt. I wanted to create all three of these Zendalas using only Mooka, just to see what sort of variations I could find!

Although I used pre-strung white, black and Renaissance tiles, I soon went 'off-piste' and ignored the strings, since I don't enjoy creating perfectly symmetrical patterns – I prefer my designs to be more free-flowing. One thing that is immediately evident in these Zendalas is that the white gel pen is far thicker than the Micron 01 pen and lends itself to a less detailed approach. These tiles look quite different, partly because of the background colour and also because of the amount of detail in the tangling.

I have created step-outs for three versions of Mooka to help Zentangle enthusiasts who have had difficulties with this tangle to draw all the variations of it, infurled and unfurled.

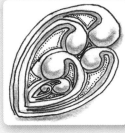

Version 1

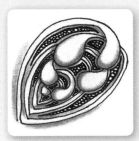

Version 2

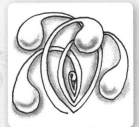

Version 3

This Zendala was created with a black Micron pen, which can describe fine detail.

For the Zendala shown left, I used a white Gelly Roll pen on a black pre-strung tile.

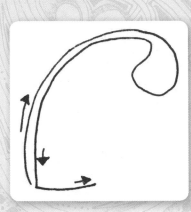

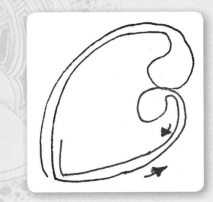

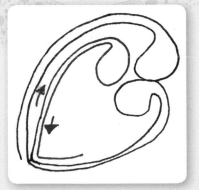

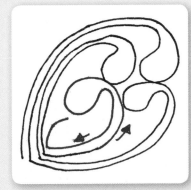

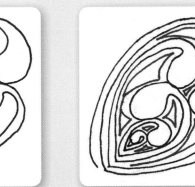

VERSION 1:
Mooka infurled, no overlaps, one continuous line

This is the place to begin learning Mooka, because there are no overlaps in the 'pods', which means that it can be drawn as one continuous line. After you have drawn the outer pods on the left and then on the right the pods diminish until the space inside is filled. Although the step-outs are spread over eight stages here, you can see that there is actually just one long line which goes in different directions.

To finish off the pattern, I like to infill the spaces between the lines of the pods, simply following the curves that are there already. In this example I also added a line of fine dots and some shading – as I did in my Zendalas, too.

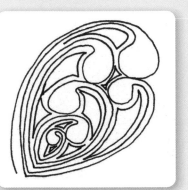

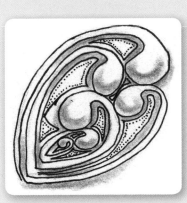

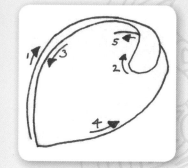
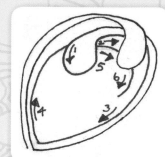
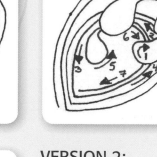
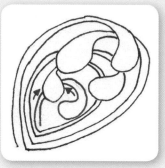

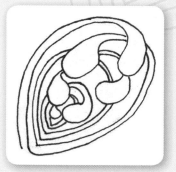

VERSION 2:
Mooka infurled, overlapping, broken line

I recommend having a go at this infurled version of Mooka next, as it will make it much easier to progress to the unfurled version. This time, after the first pod is drawn, the next one goes behind it and subsequent ones go behind both of them, which makes them more complicated to draw as you progress inwards.

So, the continuous line from Version 1 becomes an imagined continuous one, as you now have to lift your pen and then place it down on the other side of the pod to begin again. Once you get this idea of drawing one pod behind another, you just keep going until you have filled the space within the first two outer pods.

Again, there is usually space to add infills between the pods, simply following their curves. This time I filled the spaces with the Zentangle pattern Tipple, which is really useful for helping to draw something like this together. Finally I shaded it, in a slightly different way to Version 1.

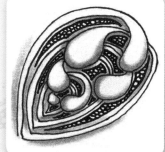

This mandala is drawn on a pre-strung Renaissance tile, using brown and sepia Micron pens.

VERSION 3: Mooka unfurled

This version of Mooka is a natural progression from the previous ones. In order to create an unfurled mooka, after the first pod the subsequent ones go behind each other, as in Version 2. Again you can only imagine the continuous line being created – in reality it is a broken line, which has to go behind those pods that are closer to the front.

I decided not to infill the spaces in the final step-out pattern for this version, so that it is easier to see the finished result. It also demonstrates better how shading really brings the finished tangle to life.

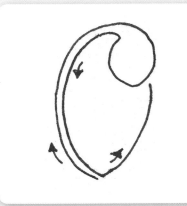
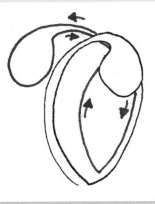

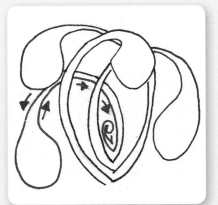
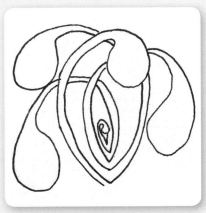

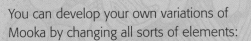

I hope that these Zendalas and step-outs help people to develop their confidence to tangle more with Mooka, as it is a very satisfying and beautiful tangle to draw. It keeps you very focused, and you gain so many of the benefits of Zentangle from drawing it, such as patience; relaxation; confidence; development of hand-eye co-ordination; and sheer happiness!

You can develop your own variations of Mooka by changing all sorts of elements:

- The width or length of each long pod.
- The size of the 'bulb' on the end of a pod – it could be tiny or enormous.
- The numbers of pods in each Mooka.
- The patterns and colours you choose to infill the gaps between the pods.
- The way you shade the finished Mooka.

I would love to see any Mooka patterns that people complete, so please feel free to email me a photo at lesley@theartsoflife.co.uk, or post them on the Facebook page that some of my students set up for me in 2014, The Arts of Tangling.

Go with the flow!

Here I created something a little different, using a Dreamweaver Unicorn stencil. I started with the unicorn in the middle – I did not tangle it, merely coloured it with a lilac Copic marker and blacked out some of the mane and tail.

I then drew a series of pencil lines across and around the unicorn to create shapes. After doing this you can then decide which tangle you want to use. The tangles here are Btl Joos, Howda and Steps, with a bit of Joy in three places. Don't think about how you want it to turn out – just do the tangles, add lines as you need them and be open-minded about where the drawing takes you.

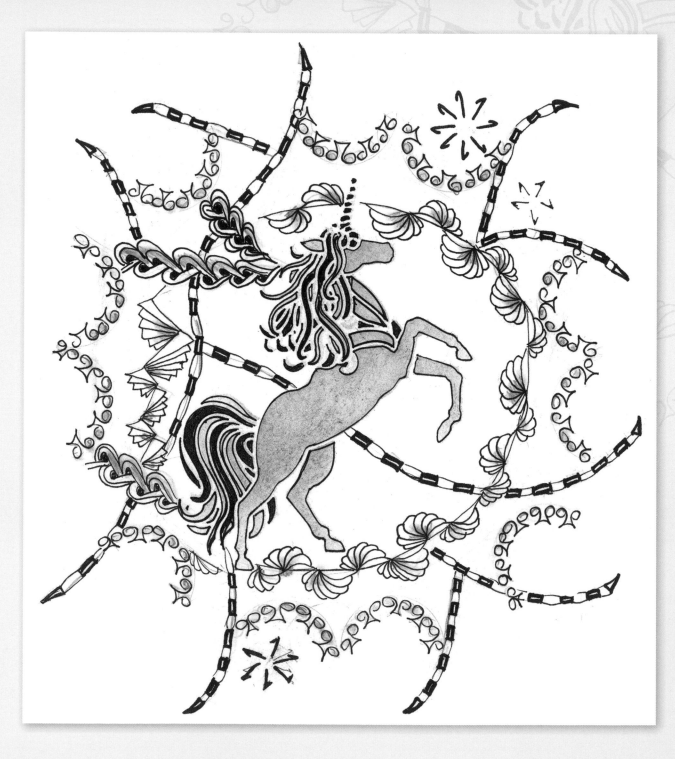

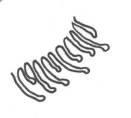

QUABOG

This tangle by Rick Roberts and Maria Thomas does not need much explanation. In the illustration I have coloured the background with Distress Ink, using an Inkduster brush. In the centre is part of the Dreamweaver unicorn stencil.

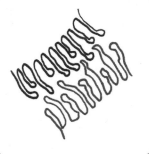

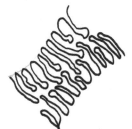

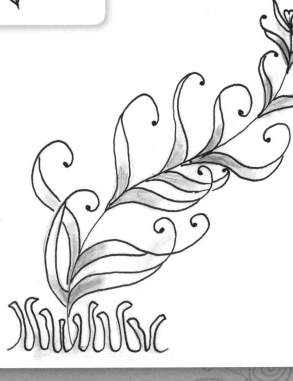

In the top illustration the tangles used are Flux, Poke Root, Printemps, Quabog and Tipple; the lower one is Quabog with Curly Bracket Feather.

Colouring in

You may not have done any colouring in since you were a child, but today it's very popular with adults too. It can be quite meditative and very calming, and there's lots of enjoyment to be had in choosing the colours. Here I have used one of Barbara Gray's Clarity stamps, available from http://www.claritystamp.co.uk, which lends itself well to a Zendala. I did not tangle the fairy, instead taking my time to colour him in with Copic markers (Promarkers are similar but with finer points). I drew a circle around him with my protractor then moved it down slightly at the top to make an inner line in which to draw Btl Joos. I created a highlight by leaving a gap where the white paper shows through (this can also be done by using a white Gelly Roll pen on top of the black). I then drew Matuvu all around the edge and carefully shaded it for a more pleasing look. You might like to add some colour of your choice to the area between the perimeter and the fairy stamp.

Red and white Zendala

I like the effect of a bit of red in a mainly black Zendala. You can experiment with the amount of red you put in. The tangles used here are Flux, N'Zeppel, Onion Drops, Printemps, Tipple, Tortuca and Web.

Pre-strung Zendalas

While you will probably enjoy drawing your own strings, you can also buy pre-strung Zendalas with several designs by Rick and Maria from www.zentangle.com. All you need to do is fill in the spaces with tangles of your choice. Here I have used an Onion Drops variation in the middle and N'Zeppel and Steps alternated. The die-cut butterflies are tangled with Arukas, Fassett and Barberpole variation.

Flower Zendala

I started with a circle for the overall size and then added a circle in the centre, in which I drew the 'flower' with a compass. I added triangles going around the flower in the middle, using a ruler, then put in further triangles behind them. The final triangles extended to the original pencil circle, which I then erased. I added some colour with a Promarker. The tangles used are Bales, Cubine, Florz, N'Zeppel, Paradox, Tipple and Sparkle on the flower in the middle.

Creating a picture

Because we associate a beautiful natural landscape with peace and calm, designs featuring elements of the natural world tend to convey the same effect. I drew this tree and then had fun filling it with tangles. The only circular shape is the moon behind the tree with a couple of the branches across it. I used a Dreamweaver stencil for the toadstools.

For your own design, draw a basic shape for a tree, add some branches and tangle away. Some of the tangles included here are Nipa, Shattuck, Snails, Onion Drops, Printemps and Poke Root, with Zingers, Poke Root, Poke Leaf and Steps hanging off the branches. I have added a little Distress Ink on the moon.

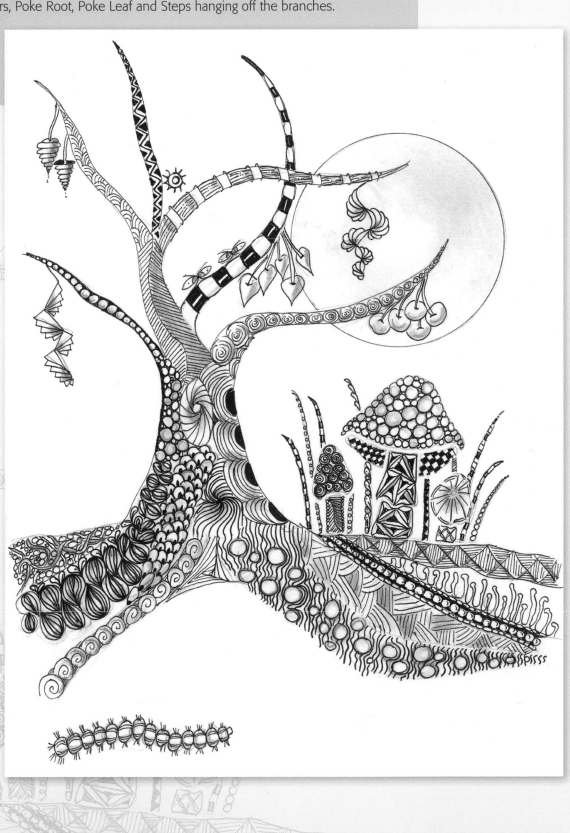

Zentangle friends: Rita Nikolajeva, CZT

Rita is multi-talented – she is an artist and also an interpreter of many languages. Originally from Latvia, she works in Belgium. I already thought I was very lucky when she agreed to do a Zendala for my book and when eight of them arrived I couldn't believe how wonderful they were. Rita has used some of her own very clever tangles and while most of us would find it hard to reach her standard it is certainly inspirational to see and admire them. Rita has provided in-depth instructions on what she has done for each one and has also offered us an insight into her methods and ideas. Below, I have stepped-out her beautiful tangle LaCePa.

The mandalas are all tangled on 220gsm (135lb) Canson paper, from which I punched circles with a 7.5cm (3in) round Artemio punch. The paper is good quality but cheaper than using original Zendala tiles, thus great for a quick meditation or for trying out tangles and techniques.
I like this size as it forces you to keep the design simple, with just a few tangles and a basic composition. I often don't even need a string. Sometimes I start in the central area by drawing a focus tangle and then radiating outwards, or I might begin at the outer edge and work inwards. If I use a string at all, it's mostly a circle traced around some object I have to hand, such as a plastic bottle cap.
In some mandalas, I use a Koh-i-Noor Magic Pencil 3400 with multicoloured lead – four colours arranged in a chequerboard manner. I think it's a very Zen method of colouring, as you don't choose the actual colour – it will change all by itself depending on the usage of the lead, the paper surface and so on.

LaCePa by Rita Nikolajeva

Shown here is a step-out of LaCePa, one of the tangles Rita used in her Zendala artwork on page 34.

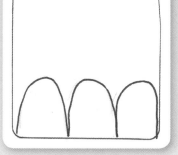
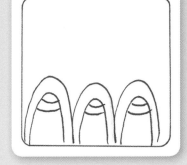
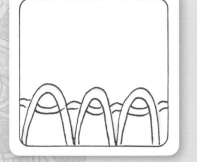
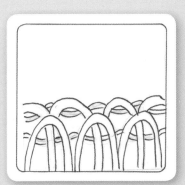

Using a Sakura Micron 01 pen and a graphite pencil for shading, I started with Showgirl (a variation of LaCePa) in the centre and worked outwards, without any strings. The other tangle used is Quipple.

For the string, I drew a circle free-hand close to the outer edge. I used a Sakura Micron 01 pen for line work, a graphite pencil for shading and a Koh-i-Noor Magic Pencil 3400 for colouring. The tangles are Matuvu and Lampions.

This mandala was created with a Sakura Micron 01 pen and a graphite pencil for shading. For the string, I traced a water-bottle cap three times, overlapping the circles.

The tangles used are Static plus Perfs in the circles, Sanibelle in the overlapping sections and Quipple with blackened spaces at the border. I also blackened the centre.

There was no string for this mandala. I started with the tangle Showgirl in the centre, then added Aura around the outer edge and a black pearl in the centre. I used a variation of my tangle LaCePa and coloured in the spaces between the 'bands'.

Here I used the Micron pen along with a Faber-Castell Pitt artist pen (Cold Grey III) for shading. There are no strings. I started with a border of my tangle Borbz around the edge, added Borbz in the centre and connected it to the border by Aurabridge. I added some Tipple as a filler all around.

With the Micron pen and a graphite pencil for shading, I started with Crescent Moon at the outer edge, then used Hollibaugh embellished with dots. I finished by filling alternate sections with Printemps. Again there were no strings.

Without any strings, I started with the tangle Showgirl in the centre, then added arcs around in two layers, crossing them in Hollibaugh-style, and finished with Quipple around the edge. I used a Koh-i-Noor Magic Pencil 3400 for the colouring.

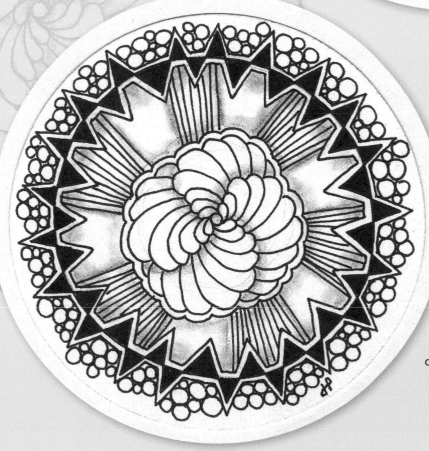

For the string, I traced the bottom of a goblet, making the base line of Rain. I added Tipple on the outer edge of Rain and used Showgirl with Aura in the centre. The connections are just radiating stripes.

Celtic knots

This isn't a tangle as such but it is fun to do and to add to your Zentangle art. I found it challenging, but on YouTube.com you will find 21 very helpful videos on Celtic knots by David Nicholls. David is a great tutor, so have a go! Here is one of the easier designs, called Fish Entrails. I didn't get it right the first time, so be patient with your own attempts.

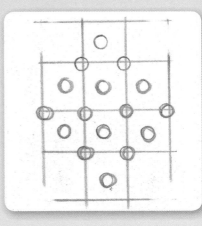 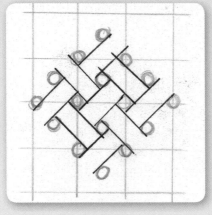 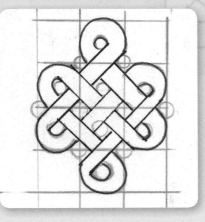

First draw a grid and then put your circles in – use a pencil as these lines will be erased later.

Next, take your pen and draw the 'weave' lines as shown.

Follow the weave lines and round them off at the corners to give a natural effect, then erase all your pencil guidelines.

I have shaded this Celtic knot in pencil and then coloured the background with a Koh-i-Noor Magic Pencil.

Stained-glass effect

Here I have used some die-cut church window designs. The first one has a star shape cut out, but this could just be drawn in. I have divided up each window and drawn many different tangles in each section, colouring them with Copic markers. The tangles used in the large window are Onamato, Shattuck, Tipple, Cadent, Fassett, Flux, Printemps, N'Zeppel, Keeko, Cubine, Heartrope and Poke Root. The medium window is Fassett with some of the triangle coloured in and the small one is N'Zeppel, always very effective.

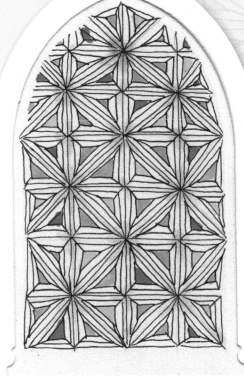

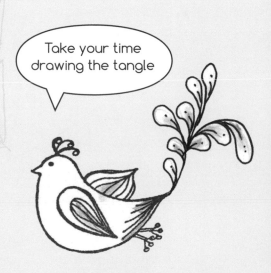

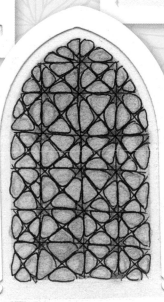

Take your time drawing the tangle

Triangle mandala

Using triangles in a mandala provides an interesting geometric contrast with the circular shape. I started this mandala with a square in the middle and then, using my triangle template, I started forming triangles that overlaid each other until I had three 'circles' of triangles. For the third circle I added a halo, doing Braze on the inside and small circles in the halo. The other tangles used are Arukas and Sanibelle.

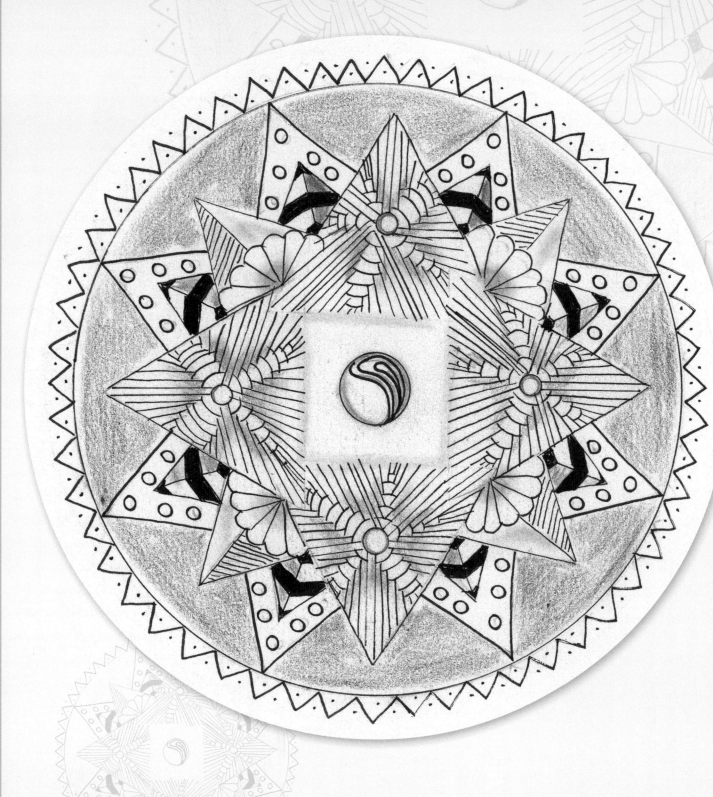

Star-shaped Zendala

Stars often feature in Zendalas. I used a star template for this one as stars are not particularly easy to draw, though you can create the Star of David with two triangles. The tangles I used are Matuvu around the outside of the circle and Auraknot for the centre of the star; a Meer variation forms the star points and a variation of Coral Seeds is between them.

Black and white Zendala

This is a very simple Zendala, using a protractor to draw the outline. If you have a protractor with cut-out smaller circles in it, draw some of them in a circle – I have used different sizes here. You can also draw them freehand. The centre is part of a KalaDalas stencil (see p.44). The tangles used are a variation of Howda (adding a small circle on top), while the circles are Cruffle with some stalks added and a bit of Flux for the leaves.

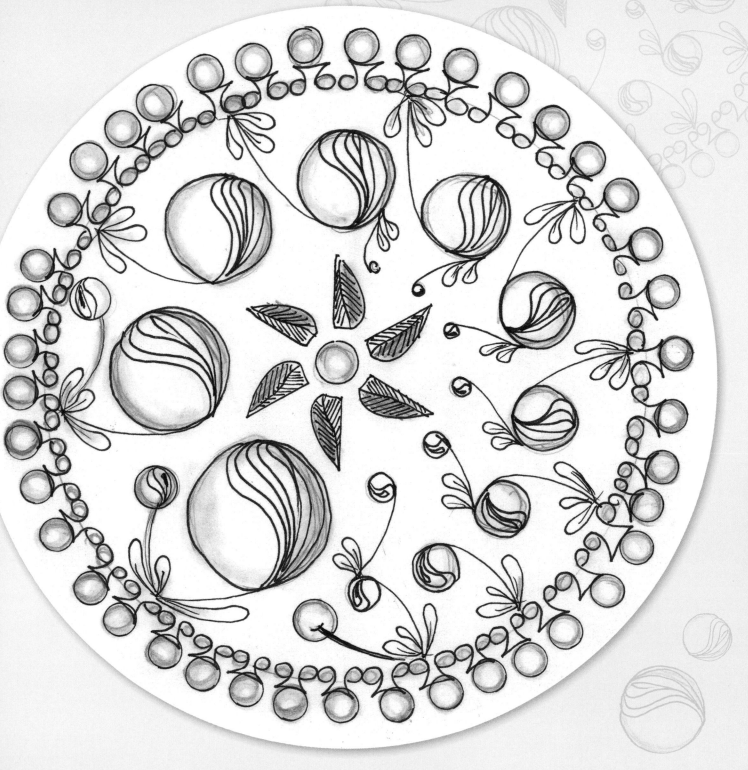

Mandala with colour

This mandala is quite complex. I started by drawing squares within squares, the third one turned round so that the corners touch the sides of the previous square. I drew a circle inside that square and then went with the flow, adding half circles on the sides of the square. Then I set about tangling it, finishing by adding some colour and mounting it on a piece of lilac card.

The tangles used are, in the middle, Hollibaugh, Knase variation and Copada, with a simple border around the edge.

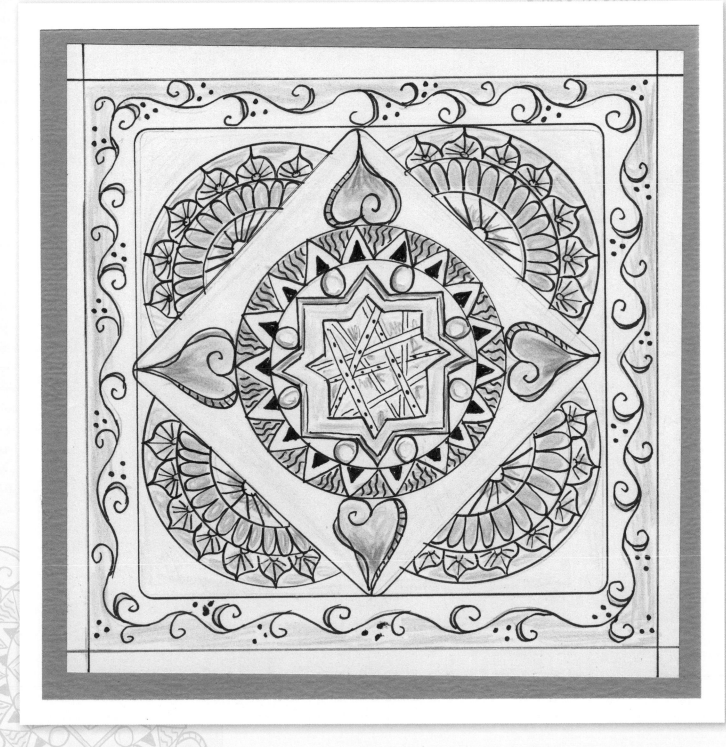

Using an apple corer

One of the things you can use to create a 'stencil' for a Zendala is an apple corer. Mine has twelve sections, though some have only eight. For the top Zendala I used all twelve sections and alternated Emingle and scrolled Feathers with a bit of colour. In the second one I used every other section and tangled with Copada and Avreal. The third Zendala is drawn using two adjacent sections and leaving the next one out. It is tangled with Pia, using a purple fineliner.

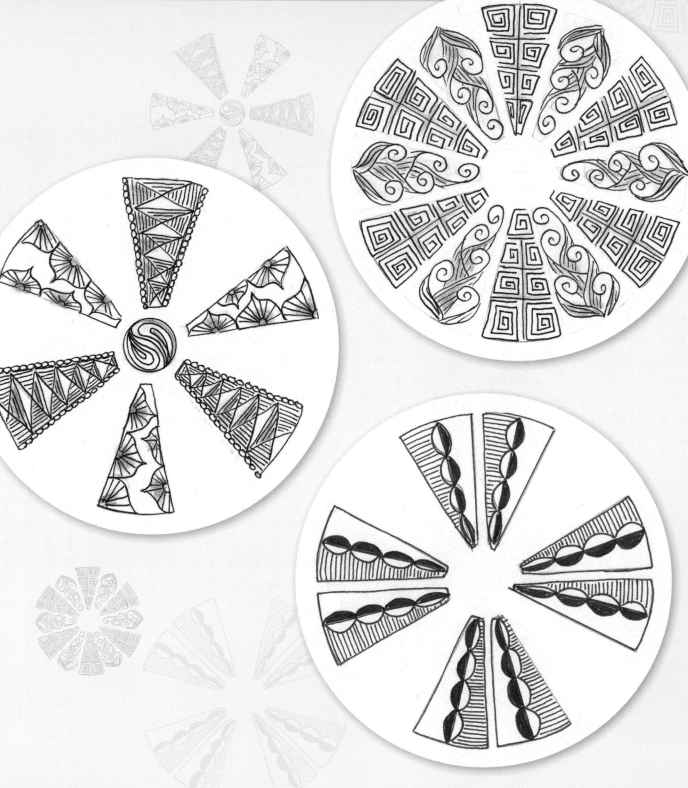

Decagon Zendala

A die-cutting machine allows you to cut out a wide range of shapes quickly and accurately, so if you are keen on papercraft you will find one a good investment. I used a decagon die to cut this shape. It is easy to use for tangling as the shape can be divided up easily from point to point. The tangles here are Thorns variation and N'Zeppel.

Using stencils

There are various brands of stencil available, such as Stamposaurus and Crafter's Workshop, offering many different designs. KalaDalas Stencils by Julie Evans CZT are easy to use and can be obtained direct from Julie at www.etsy.com/shop/KalaDalasStencils. The design shown here comes from a pack called 5-piece Sampler, available in both 9cm (3½in) and 11.5cm (4½in) sizes. They are lightweight vinyl stencils, much cheaper than metal ones, but less robust, so take more care when using them. Here I used Bales, Paradox around the outside, Flux and Tipple inside and Florz variation in the middle.

Stencils with background colour

For the artworks shown on this page I started by applying colour through some stencils with Ink Dusters and Distress Inks. I then used one of the KalaDalas stencils from the 5-piece Sampler set, tracing through the outlines in pencil and then tangling various parts of the stencil to create three different effects. To make your own designs, erase any pencil lines when you have finished and then shade your design either with a graphite pencil or with coloured pencils. You can use all or just part of the stencil as I have done.

The tangles are: first image, Paradox; second image, Dandi and Flux variation; third image, Dragonair and N'Zeppel.

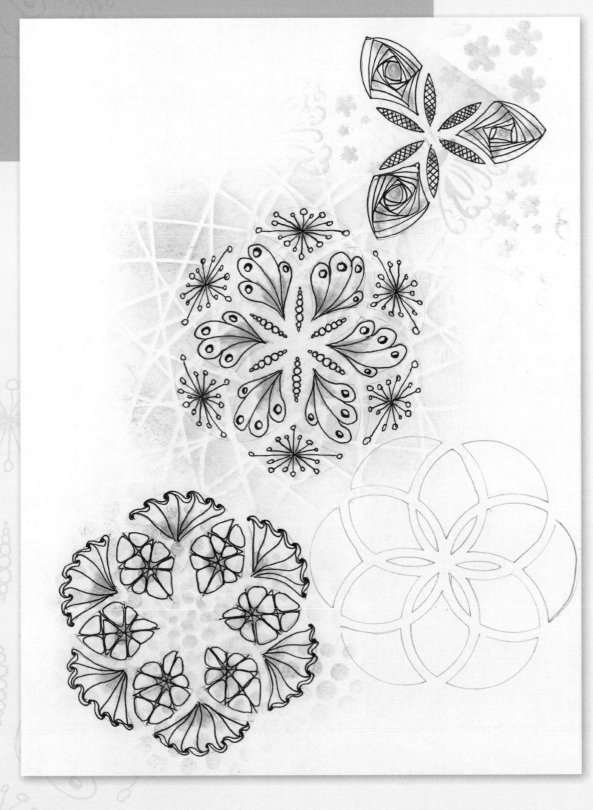

Background colour

I cut out these owl shapes with a die-cutting machine. Before lifting the die off the shape, I used an Inkylicious Ink Duster brush with some Tim Holtz Distress Inks to add colour to the finished shape. Claritystamp also do a very good set of four stencil brushes, or you can use a piece of make-up sponge and an ink pad for the same effect. Once the die was removed a white edge to the shape was revealed. I used Spellbinders owl dies and also a star stencil in the background.

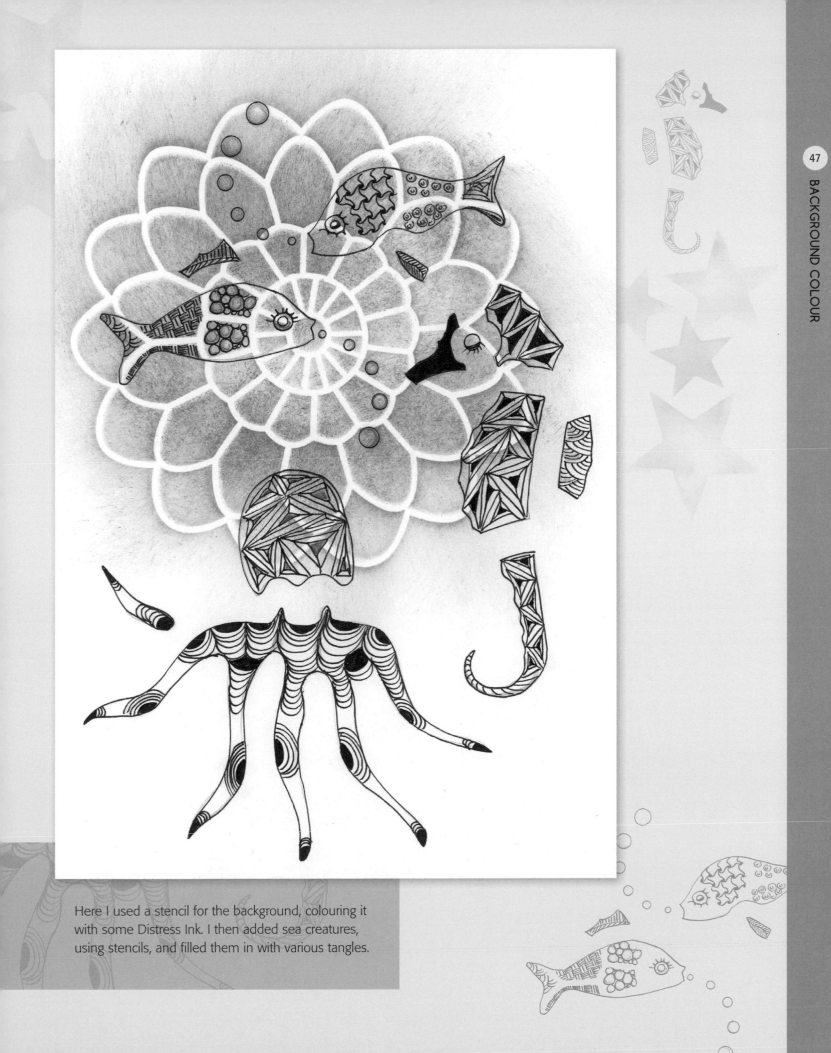

Here I used a stencil for the background, colouring it with some Distress Ink. I then added sea creatures, using stencils, and filled them in with various tangles.

Background colour (continued)

This page was created by first colouring some inexpensive snowflake stencils with Distress Inks. I then used part of a KalaDalas Demo Stencil (these are quite big).

The centre is tangled with Auseklis, and next to that there is Copada and Dandi. The outer spaces are filled with Crescent Moon and Onion Drops with a bit of Cruffle.

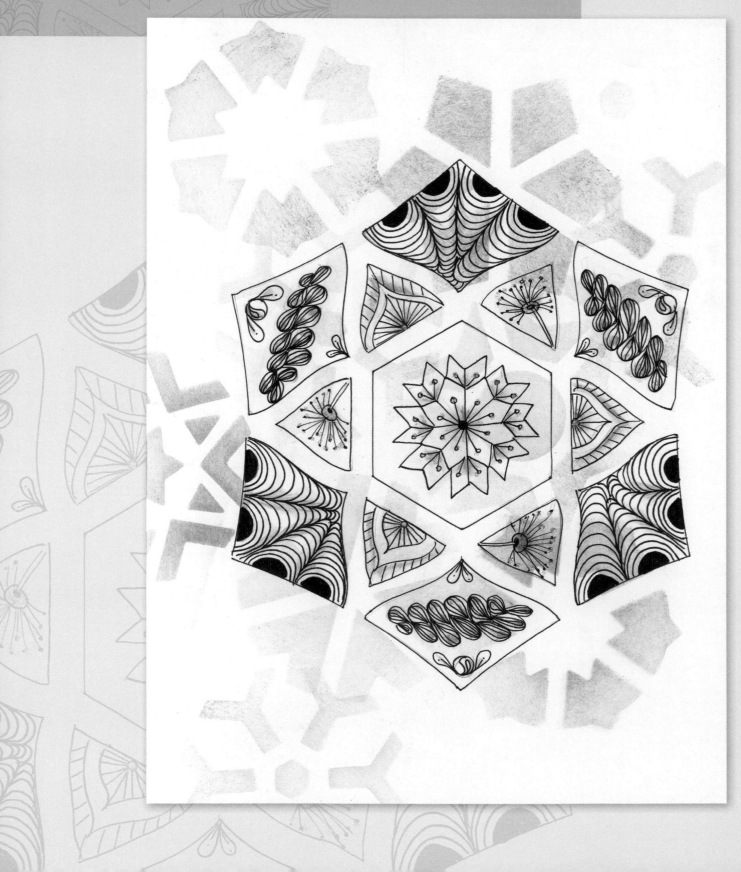

Shaving foam background colour

This is a lovely messy way of making background colour. You can buy little bottles of inks such as Posh Rainbow Ink in various colours; I also use Archival Brilliance Pearlescent inks. Alternatively, acrylic or watercolour paints will work well. Take an old tray or dish, spread cheap shaving foam over it and sprinkle a few drops of colour on the foam. With a fork or a cocktail stick, pull the colour across to make lines and then repeat in the other direction. It will look a bit like marble at this stage.

Next, take some white card or heavyweight paper and press it on to the mixture. Lift it off, scrape off the foam, then wipe with paper towel and you will find you have a lovely coloured sheet of card. You can repeat with many more pieces of card or paper, occasionally adding another drop of colour.

I have left two of these 'tiles' blank so that you can see the effect achieved with this technique – no two sheets will be the same. On the third one I have done a circle of N'Zeppel.

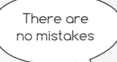

There are no mistakes

Using part of a stencil

I achieved this effect using part of the Dreamweaver elephant stencil four times in a circle to make a mandala. It is not obvious that it is the elephant unless it is pointed out. I used Btl Joos around the outside, a Meer variation on the trunk, Zander on the tusk and a bit of N'Zeppel for the head. Widget was ideal for the eye and the centre.

In the second Zendala, the whole elephant is used with the same tangles as the first, but also Cadent, Crescent Moon and Flux on the rest of the body.

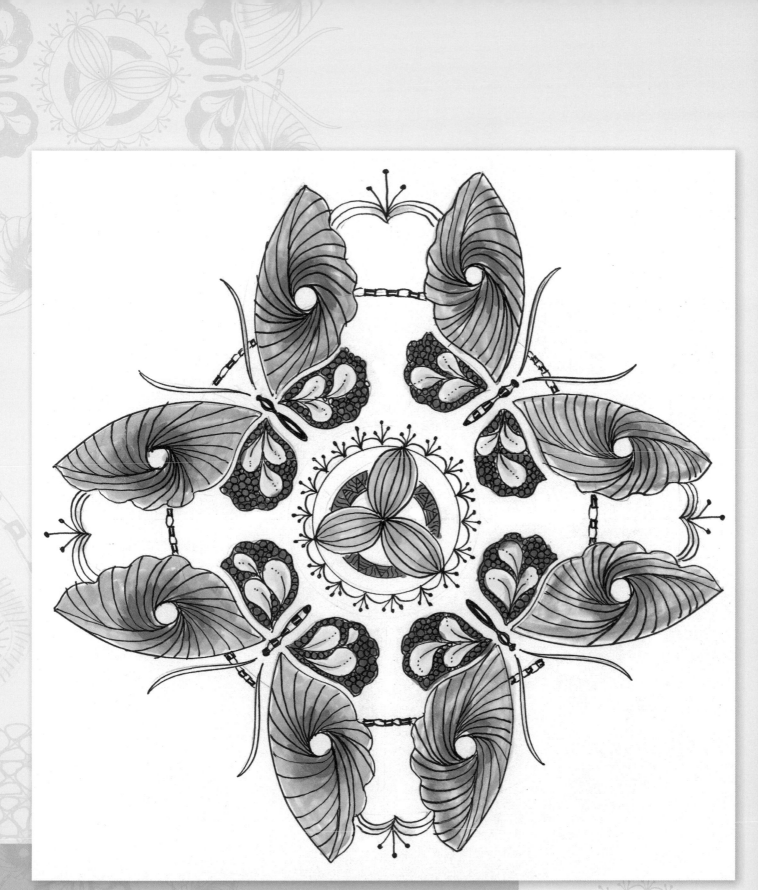

This is a Dreamweaver butterfly stencil, used four times in a circle like the elephant. Again the subject may not be obvious. The tangles used are Sparkle and Flux with Btl Joos on the body; the centre is surrounded by Puf Border.

Zentangle friends: June Bailey

This lovely Zendala was done by my friend June Bailey, who comes to my Zentangle group. She has created a beautiful, intricate seascape with clever use of colour. I have got to know June well and realize how much she gets out of her Zentangle practice. As the mother of two young boys, she needs a bit of 'me time' when she can enjoy her creativity.

Teabag folding

This miniature form of origami was originally done using decorative teabag wrappers rather than the teabags themselves. It's a delightful way of turning artwork into decorative objects, and you'll find the process of folding and watching your designs take new shapes a meditative form of papercraft. There are some complicated teabag folds, but here I have chosen a basic one. I started by photocopying June's seascape about four times and then cutting it into eight 10cm (4in) squares.

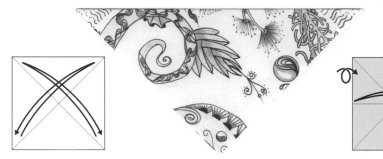

1. Fold a square diagonally and then open it up. Fold diagonally the other way and open it again.

2. Next, turn it over, fold it in half and open it up. Fold in half the other way.

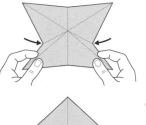

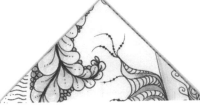

3. Fold as shown to form a triangle.

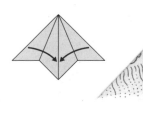

4. Fold the right-hand side down and then the left-hand side.

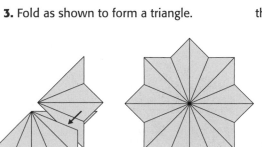

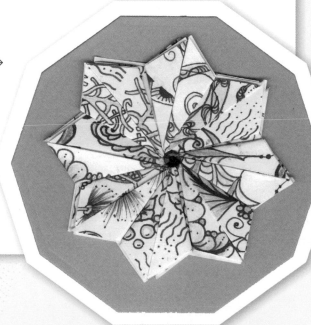

You now have the finished fold. Repeat with the remaining squares and form a flower by connecting them in a circle, using a little glue to hold them together. Adding a gem to the middle then mounting the flower on a piece of card makes a lovely card or a tag for a gift.

Rubber stamps

Using rubber stamps offers another source of designs for tangling. The first example here, using a Rubber Stampede stamp, is drawn on a Renaissance tile with a brown Micron pen and some highlights from a white charcoal pencil. The tangles used are Puf Border, Dooleedo, Auraleah, Brax and Verdigogh.

The second one, using the stamp Artprints Gracious Lady, has Puffle and circles drawn with a sepia pen.

The third example is a Paper Artsy stamp, with a Za border in brown and sepia. All of these designs would make attractive greetings cards.

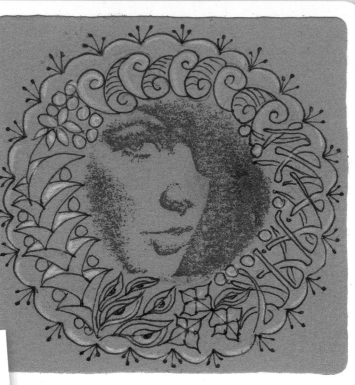

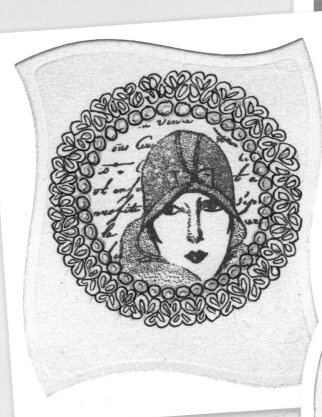

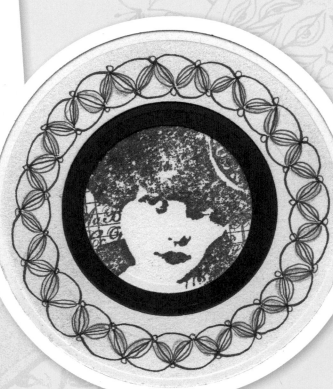

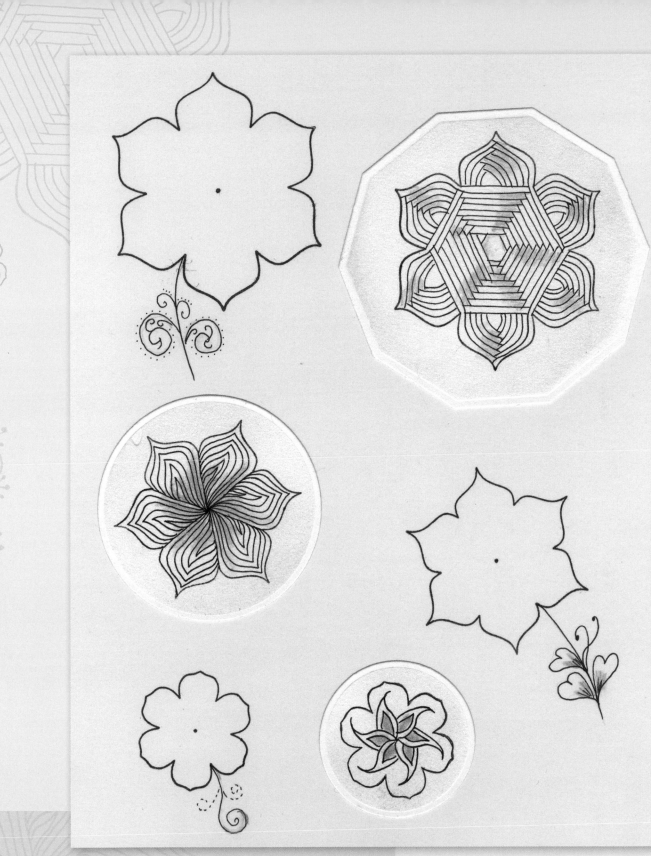

Here I have used flower designs from Dimension Stamps. They are just outline stamps, leaving a lot of scope for tangling. In the large flower I have done Auraknot. I have added stalks on the outline stamps to illustrate how you might use them along with the completed stamps. The second flower is Merryweather and on the third I have done Fengle.

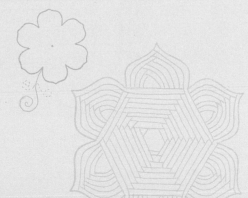

Greetings cards with numbers and letters

Tangling your own greetings cards allows you to make one-off cards to suit the occasion. I use plastic stencils to pencil in the numbers or letters, though you can draw them freehand if you prefer. I drew these designs on a piece of 250gsm white card measuring 18 x 9cm (7 x 3½in). I then folded a 21 x 19cm (8¼ x 7½in) piece of coloured card in half to make a card blank measuring 19cm x 10.5cm (7½ x 4⅛in) and stuck the white card onto this. However, the size doesn't matter as long as it fits in an envelope.

The first one is similar to a birthday card I made last year for someone reaching the age of 105. I have used Cruffle in the left-hand corner. Number one is Crescent Moon, the zero is Flux and the number five is Fassett. I have added some Steps running across as well as Btl Joos and some Poke Root.

The second card is like one I did for my grandson, Tom. The T is Heartrope and Crescent Moon with a Zinger hanging down and a Puf border at the top; the O is Poke Root, Tipple and some Poke Leaf; the M is Zander, Bales, Btl Joos and N'Zeppel. There is a Morning Glory vine running behind.

Both of these cards were coloured with my Koh-i-Noor Magic Pencil and mounted on a coloured card.

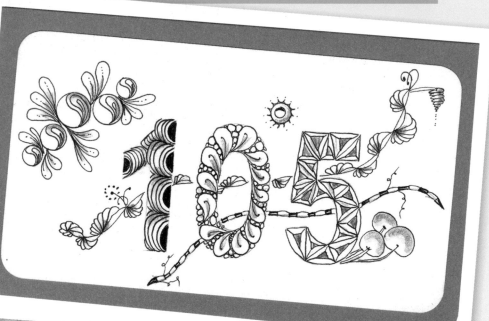

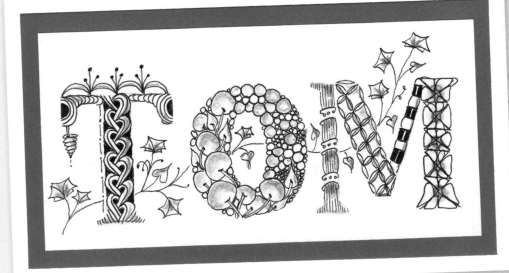

Cards for any occasion

The three little cards here are very versatile and take only minutes to make. The first one is created using die-cut flowers and tangling with Marbaix; the second is done on a Zentangle tile with Cruffle flowers and Verdigogh stems; the third one is done on blue card with a white Gelly Roll pen. The blue card was die cut before I drew the tangles on it.

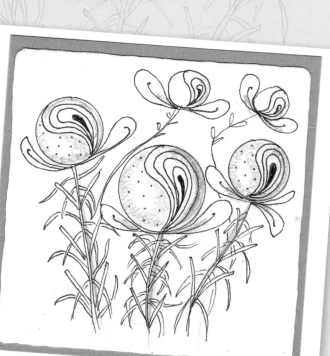

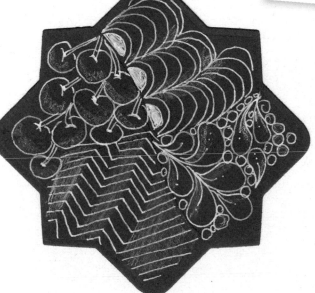

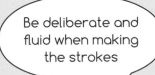
Be deliberate and fluid when making the strokes

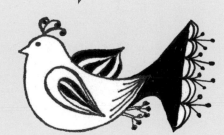

Making a concertina card

This is a lovely project to complete. I cut a piece of lilac card in half lengthwise and then folded it into a concertina – one 'valley' fold and then a 'mountain' fold and so on.

Starting with the cover, I used a decagon die-cut shape and drew Paradox with a purple sparkle Gelly Roll pen. I added a gem in the middle. On the inside the first page is part of a Dreamweaver stencil, and again using a coloured pen I filled it with Onion Drops, Flux and Tipple. On the next page I made a little pocket to put a tangle in and used LaCePa and Steps on the pocket. The following page is a circle of N'Zeppel and the last page is Angel Fish, Marbaix and Widget. You could decorate the back of this too and add some pretty ribbon to tie it up.

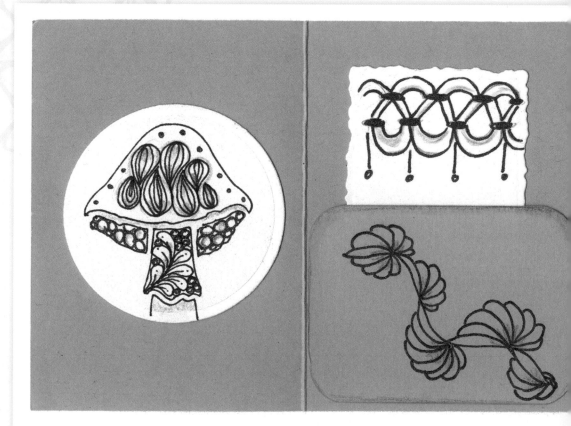

Inside pages

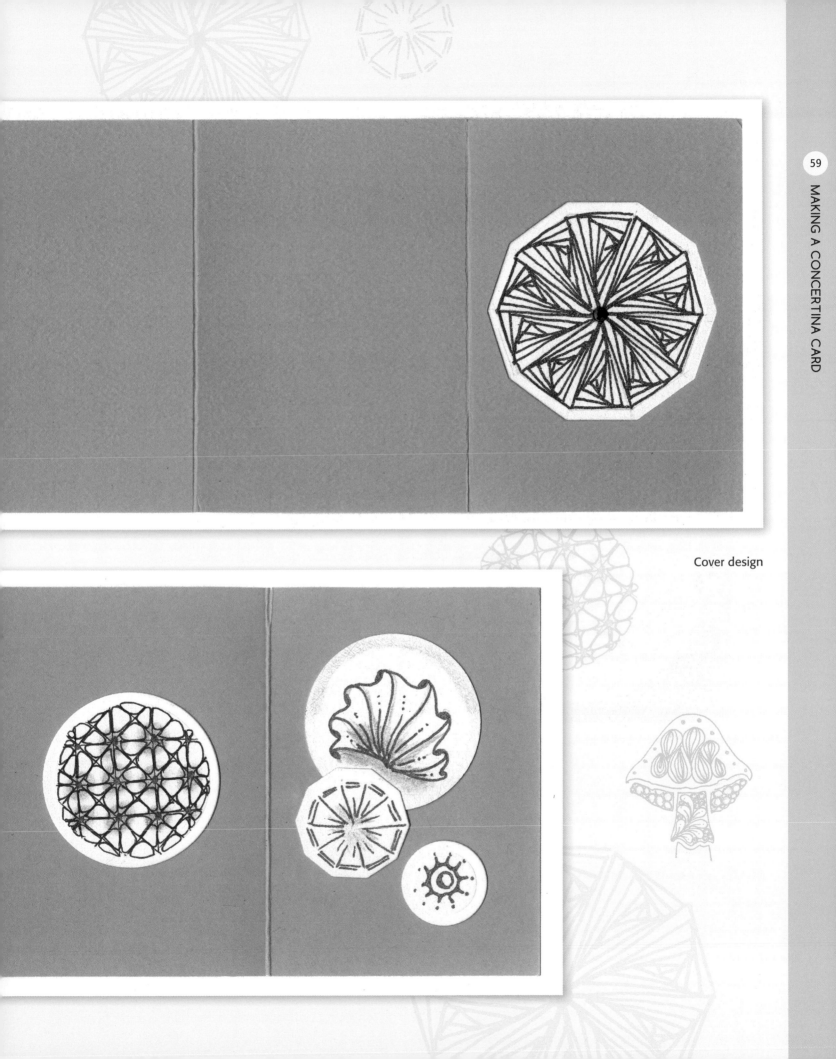

Cover design

Quick cards

These three cards are made with blank cards and each one has a Zendala drawn on some artist's paper. The first one is done using part of a stencil; the tangle is Copada. The second one is part of a KalaDalas Stencil and the tangles used are Brax in the middle, Dragonair and Tipple in the circle and Btl Joos around the outside. The third one is the tangle Chemystery in a circle. They each have a little craft gem in the centre.

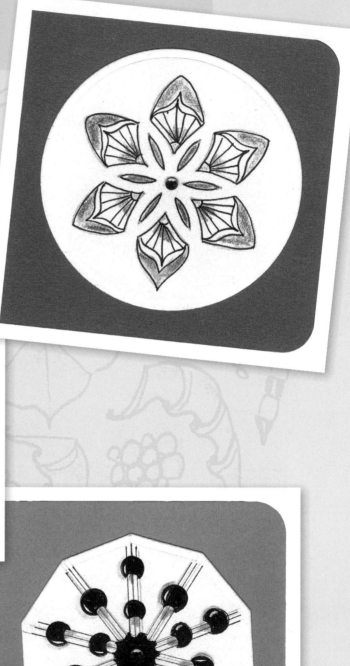

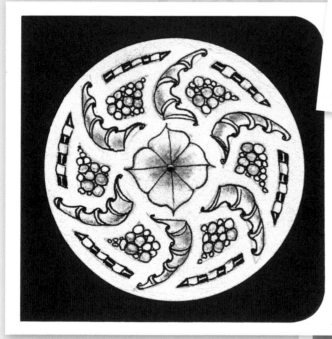

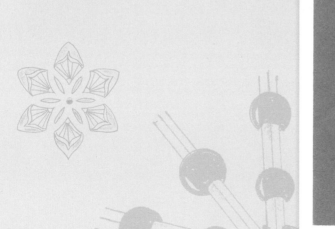

Aperture card

For this card I die-cut a circular aperture, but pre-cut aperture cards can be bought from a craft shop. I used a KalaDalas stencil on the inside of the card, inside a vase stencil. I then closed the card and carried the stencil shape on to the outside of the card, creating a complete Zendala. The idea here is that the card holds a surprise when you open it. Very few tangles appear in this design: I used Poke Root, Poke Leaf, Meer and, on the front, a little Organza border. I coloured it all with a Koh-i-Noor Magic Pencil.

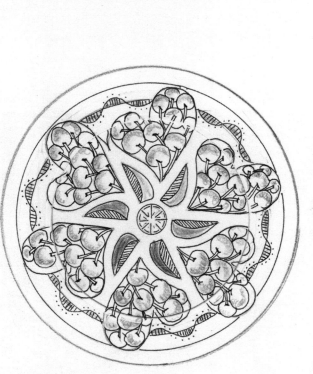

Outside

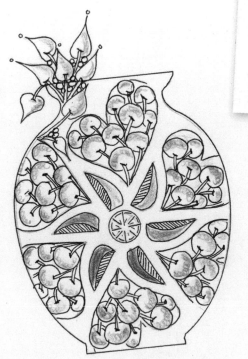

Inside

Making tags

To create a nice added touch for your gifts, make tags on which you can write a thoughtful message to the recipients – after all, they will value your warm feelings towards them as much as the gift itself. Coloured fineliners are suitable for these and glitter pens such as Sakura Gelly Roll Black Sparkle are very effective, too. Give the sparkle pens a try on coloured card as well as white.

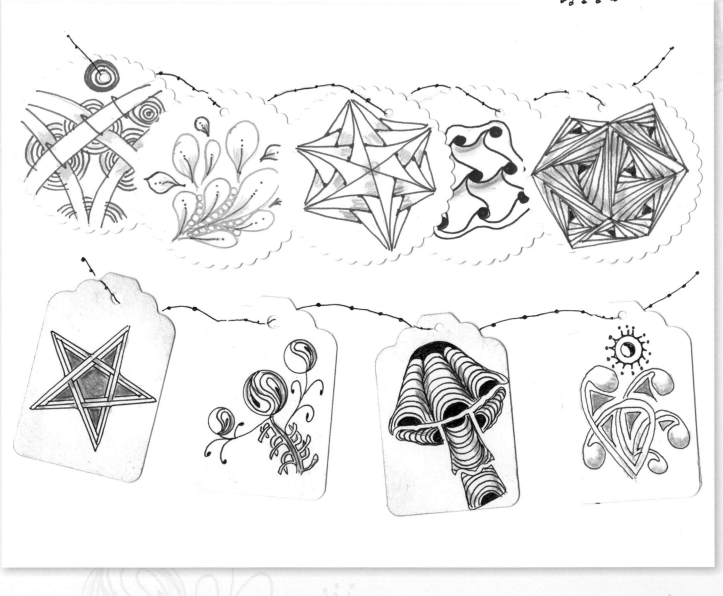

A tangle a day

One of the best things you can do for your wellbeing is to practise Zentangle every day – just ten minutes a day in a meditative frame of mind as you draw your tangles will calm and ground you. I have Carole Ohl's book *Tangle A Day Calendar* (openseedarts.blogspot.com). Below is a page from it which I tangled one evening. I just kept on adding because I found the process so relaxing; it doesn't matter that the final result is a little overdone. I used mostly Cruffle, Onion Drops and Mooka, coloured with a Koh-i-Noor Magic Pencil.

The other two tiles are examples of spending 10 minutes tangling – they are very free and easy drawings, again coloured with a Magic Pencil.

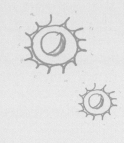

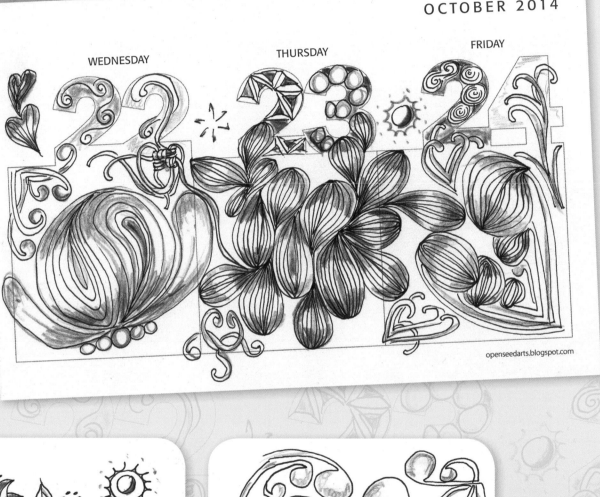

OCTOBER 2014

WEDNESDAY THURSDAY FRIDAY

openseedarts.blogspot.com

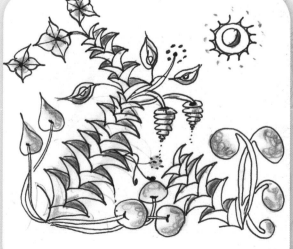

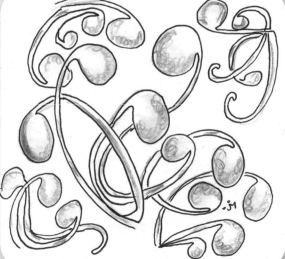

Zentangle friends: Caroline Clarke

This design is based on the compass pattern shown on p.14. It was created by one of my Zentangle group, Caroline Clarke, just using the 'petal' part and erasing the circle lines. I think it makes a lovely design and have copied the idea to make my own 'Caroline Star' (bottom). I tore the edge around my 'star' and coloured the edge before sticking it on a circle.

Caroline used Btl Joos, Crescent Moon and Tipple with a clever bit that forms a pattern joining it to the Crescent Moon. Mine is very simple, with Btl Joos and Flux with Tipple.

Zentangle friends: Iris Jones & Julia Mears

I teach a Zentangle class at a care home once a week and one of my students is Iris Jones, 88 years old and really enjoying her Zentangle sessions. The first Zendala shown here is one that Iris has done for this book using various tangles that she likes.

The second is by one of my Zentangle group, Julia Mears. Julia seems to have quite an affinity with fish and other sea life. She drew this attractive fish first before doing all the tangles around it.

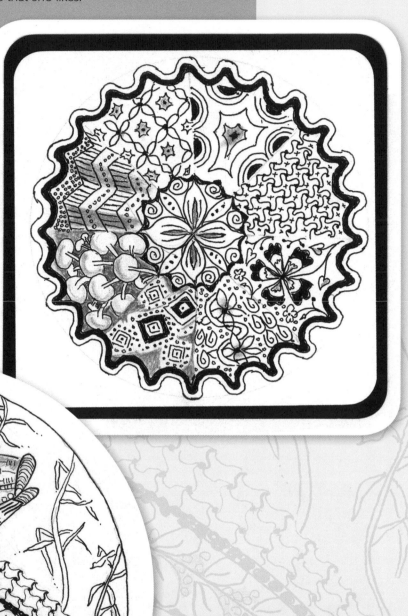

Zentangle friends: Mary Jane Holcroft

Mary Jane Holcroft is a primary school teacher and an artist too. Consequently, she has a real talent for drawing mandalas with colour.

I love the idea of a mandala representing a never-ending cycle; a repeating pattern that echoes the life pattern of the universe. We see circles all around us in nature, and with the aid of a microscope it is evident that circular structures are the building blocks of life. When I draw a mandala I create some kind of structure, some kind of order. Each repeated small segment comes together round a central point to make something more powerful, more expressive than it would be on its own. The mandala unifies.

The two circular mandalas here were created on Zentangle Zendala tiles. These tiles were pre-strung, allowing me to focus on the tangles and shading. I try to balance darker and lighter areas when tangling.

Poke Root and Betweed are the main players in this piece, complemented by Printemps and Zinger. The use of black makes the tangle 'pop'. It also helps to create an undulating effect next to the lighter Betweed.

Paradox creates the central segment here – the complexity that can be created with such a simple line always amazes me. Hypnotic, Pheasant and Crescent Moon complete the image.

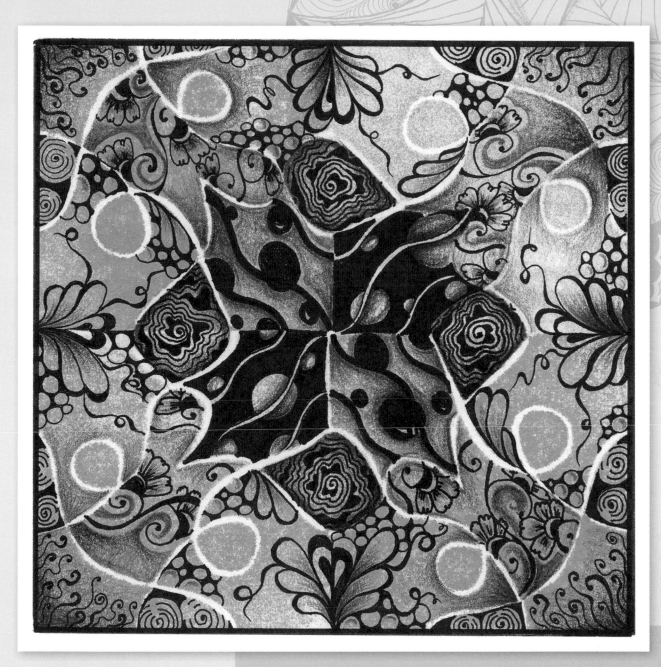

Here I used Printemps, Diva Dance, Rock and Roll, Fescu, Quipple and Henna Drum.

Fellow CZT Arja de Lange-Huisman introduced me to the squaredala technique. She cleverly created a way of printing, using foam tiles, to make an interesting background for tangles. Her blog, elefantangleblogspot.com, contains full instructions.

The pieces here and overleaf contain some of my favourite tangles: Diva Dance, Flukes and Leaflet seem to find their way into so much of my work. I love colour, so instead of shading in graphite pencil I used Derwent Inktense pencils to create depth. I simply chose slightly darker shades of the existing background colours.

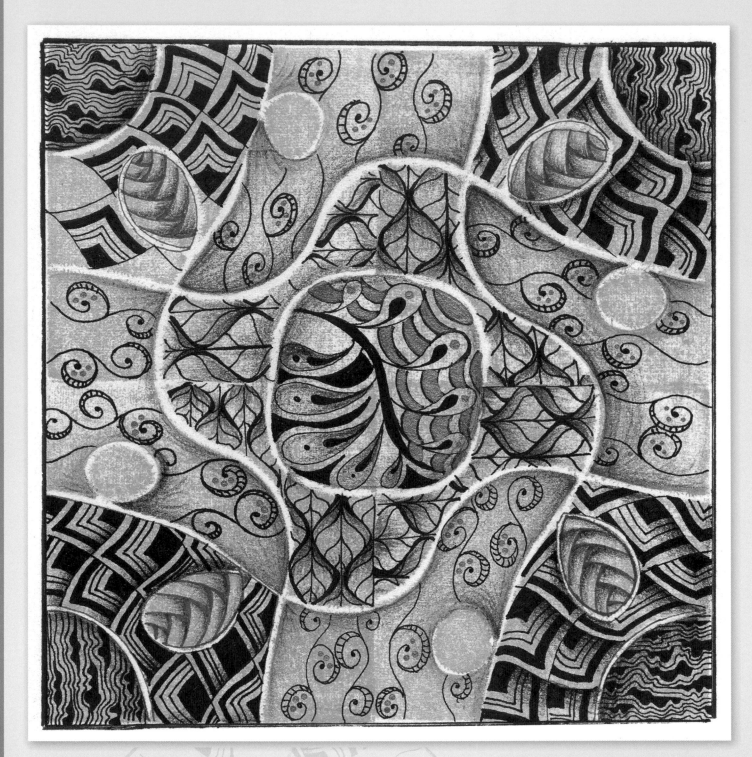

This square consists of Flukes, Diva Dance, Waltz, Betweed and Leaflet.

Tangles Galore

In the following pages you will find an array of tangles to try, with step-outs and artwork that demonstrates how you might use them. As your tangling skills grow, so will your inspiration for your own artworks, along with ideas for new tangles too.

The selection here is just a starting point in the world of Zentangle; there are many more tangles to be found on the internet, in an ever-growing library of beautiful and intricate patterns. The best sites to visit are www.zentangle.com and www.tanglepatterns.com.

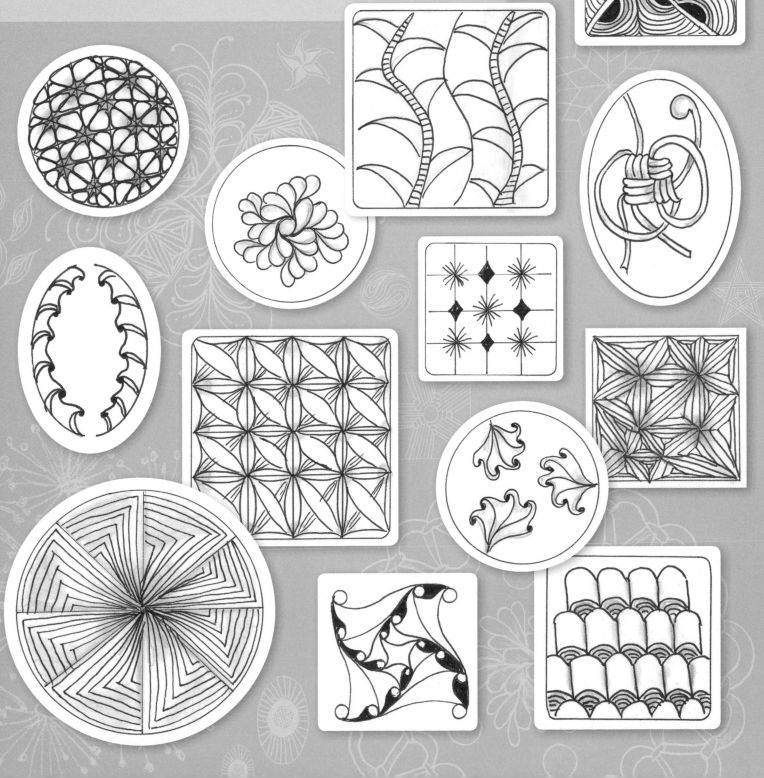

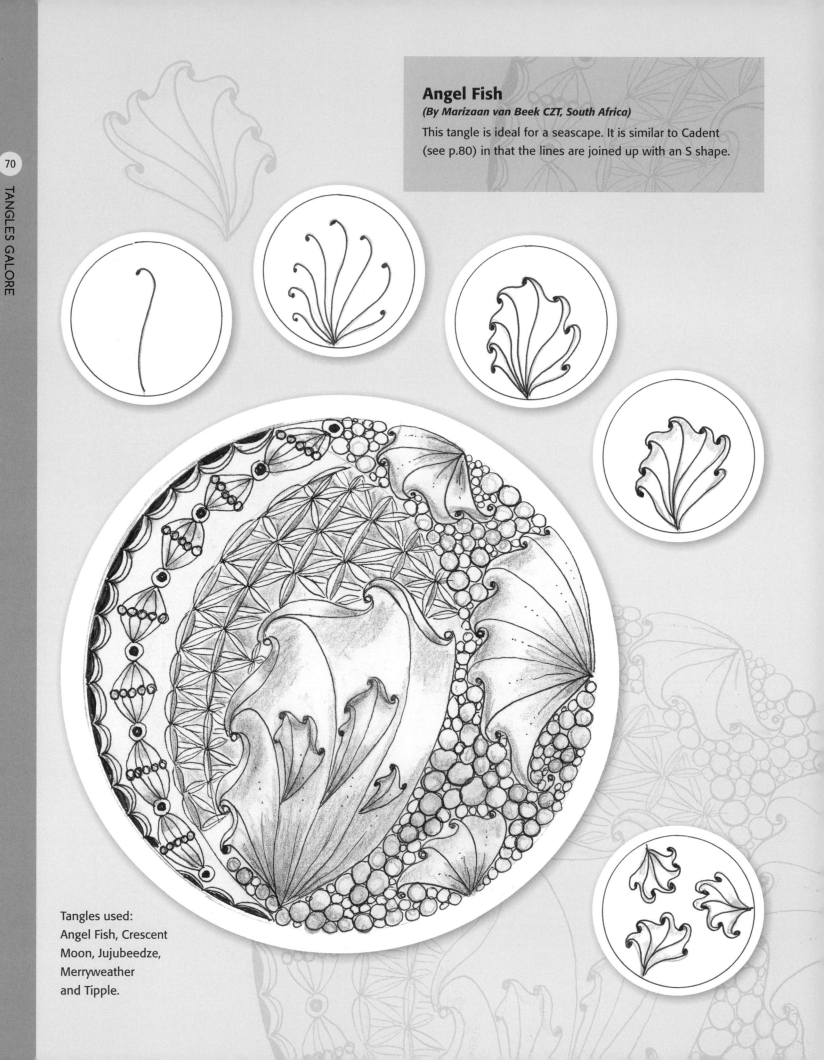

Angel Fish
(By Marizaan van Beek CZT, South Africa)

This tangle is ideal for a seascape. It is similar to Cadent (see p.80) in that the lines are joined up with an S shape.

Tangles used:
Angel Fish, Crescent Moon, Jujubeedze, Merryweather and Tipple.

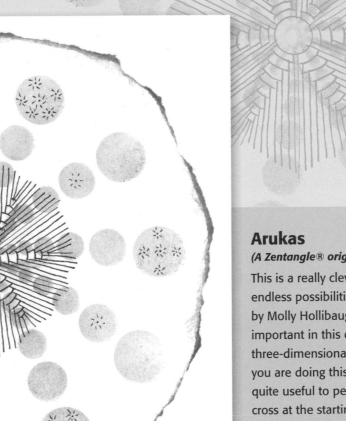

Arukas
(A Zentangle® original)

This is a really clever tangle with endless possibilities, created by Molly Hollibaugh. Shading is important in this one to add a three-dimensional feel. When you are doing this tangle it is quite useful to pencil a small cross at the starting point so that you know where you began. Rotate your piece of paper as you go, and when you have completed the lines going round once, add the second circle, then continue in the same vein.

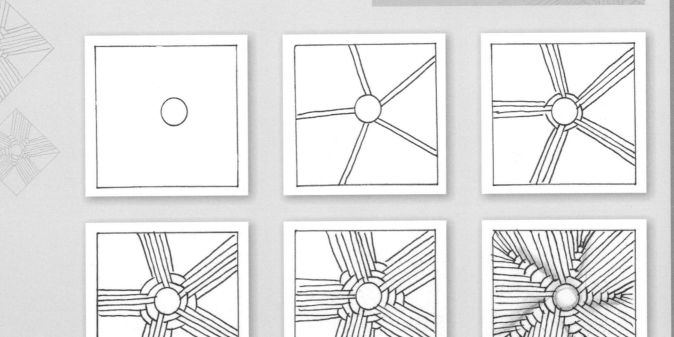

Aurabridge
(By Rita Nikolajeva CZT, Latvia)

This is not an entirely new tangle, as it is really the well-known Hollibaugh within a frame. If you look at Rita's Zendalas on p.34 you will see how she uses it. I have done three step-outs – the first as a border, the second one showing how you could use it as a different shape and the third done within a circle.

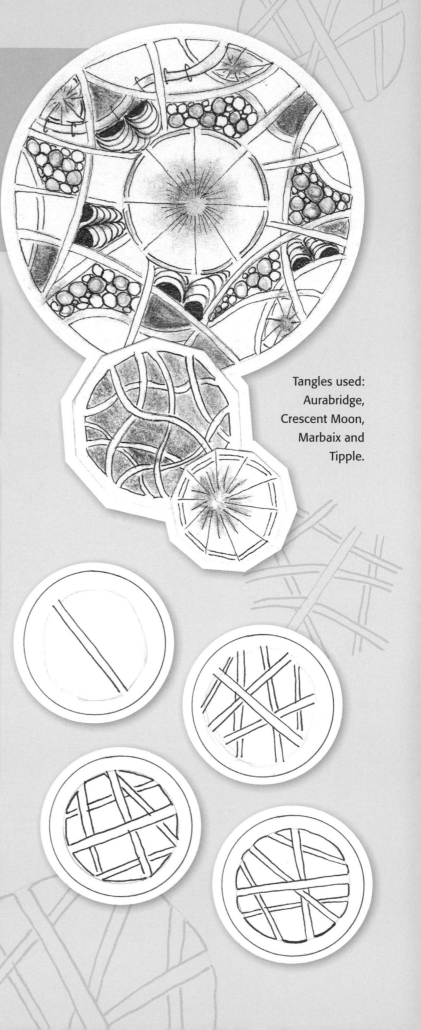

Tangles used:
Aurabridge,
Crescent Moon,
Marbaix and
Tipple.

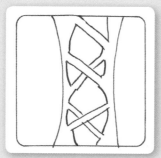
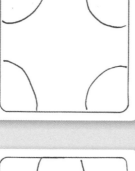
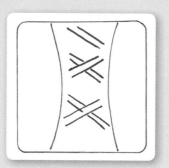
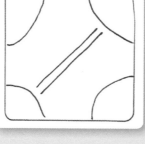
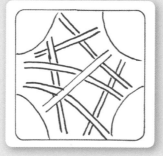
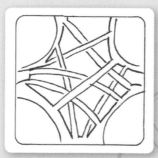
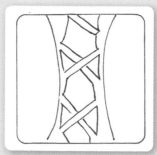
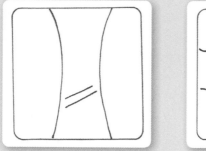

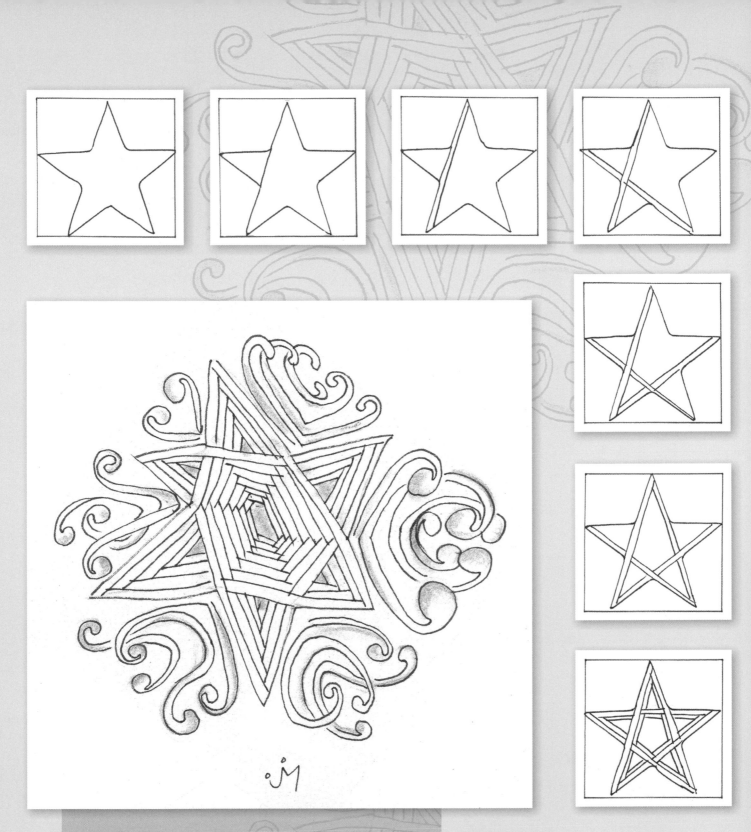

Auraknot

(A Zentangle® original)

This is quite a tricky tangle, so I used a star template to make every stroke a straight line. Once you feel confident at drawing it you can then try an irregular star shape where you can incorporate curves as well as straight lines. Keep on rotating your tile as you do each stroke until you reach the middle.

Tangles used:
Auraknot and
Mooka.

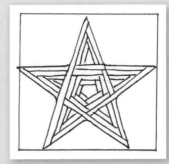

Auraleah
(By Carla de Preez, South Africa)

To draw this leafy tangle, start with a relaxed line and draw a semi-circle halfway along it on one side. On the other side, draw a more flattened semi-circle longer than the first, making sure both ends meet the line. Continue in this way, working on alternate sides and enlarging the semi-circle each time.

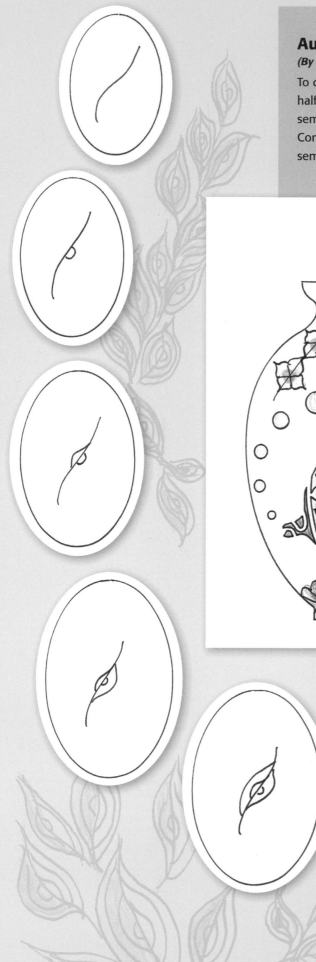

Tangles used:
Angelfish,
Auraleah, Brax,
Shattuck and
Tipple.

Auseklis
(By Rita Nikolajeva, CZT)

This tangle would make an attractive festive decoration or card. I used a Gelly Roll pen for the blue colouring.

Tangles used: on the fish, Crescent Moon, Fassett and Shattuck; beside the fish, a variation of Auseklis.

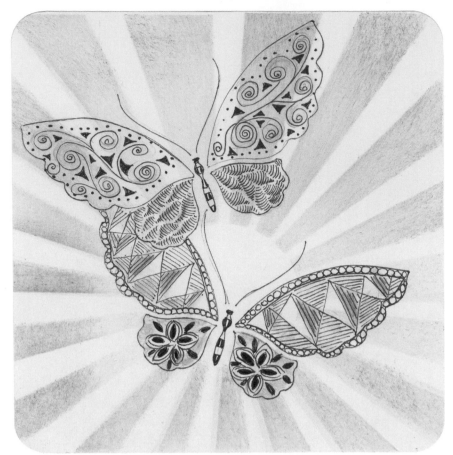

Tangles used: Ibex and
Indyrella on the top butterfly;
Avreal on the second butterfly,
with flowers on the lower wings.
Both have Btl Joos for the body.

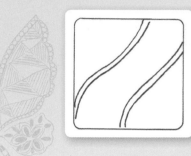

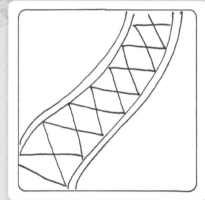

Avreal

(A Zentangle® original)

This tangle by Rick and Maria makes
a very attractive border. The butterfly
stencil is by Dreamweaver.

Hold your
writing
instrument
lightly

Bookee

(By Laura Harms CZT, Canada)
http://iamthedivaczt.blogspot.co.uk

This tangle is a pleasingly simple one to follow but very effective.
Check out Laura's blogspot for lots of ideas and challenges.

Tangles used:
Bookee and Trumpits.

Borbz

(By Rita Nikolajeva CZT, Latvia)

This great tangle from Rita looks simple but a lot of practice is required to get it looking good. Look for it in Rita's Zendala on p.34. I used a French curve as a template to get the shape for this illustration.

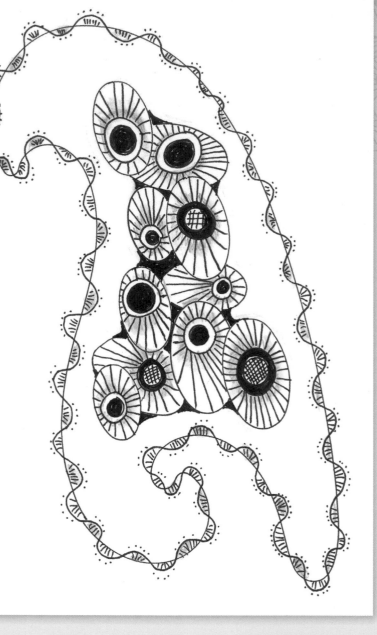

Tangles used:
Borbz and Organza.

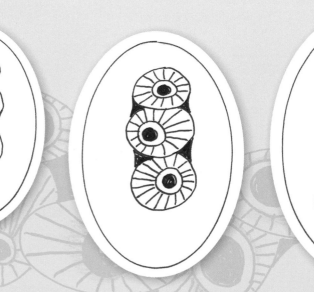

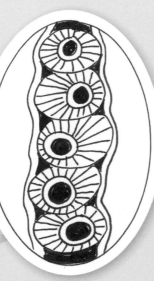

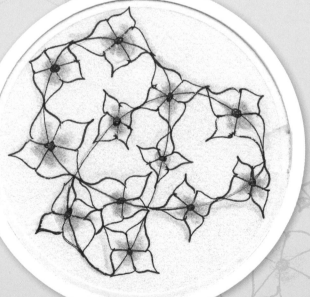

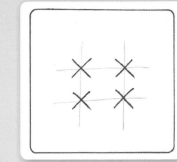

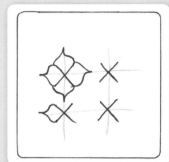

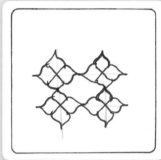

Tangles used: Brax and
Meer variation.

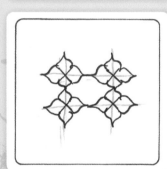

Brax

(By Helen Williams CZT, Australia)
http://alittlelime.blogspot.co.uk

This is a very pretty tangle and fairly easy. You can do it on a grid to make
it even easier, joining the 'flower' tips. Each little Brax can be used on its
own as well. It can be a lovely flowing pattern, as shown here, done
within a circle. Add colour for a different effect.

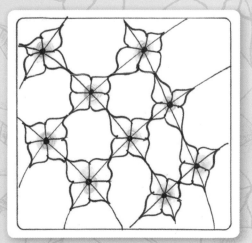

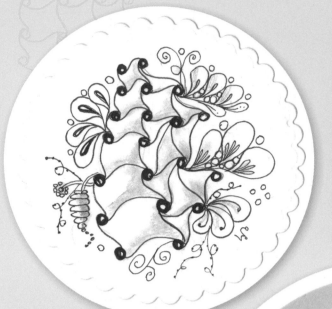

Cadent

(A Zentangle® original)

In the first illustration I started with a die-cut scalloped circle and then drew Cadent in the middle with some Flux and Zinger around it.

Below, I die-cut a circle in white card and stuck it on a larger one in blue. I started with some Cadent in the middle, drew a grid around it and turned the grid into Florz. I then added a frame with some more tangles. I did the grid in pencil and then erased the pencil after using the black pen to give a different look to the tangle.

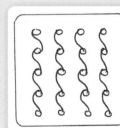

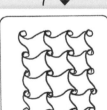

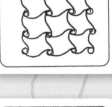

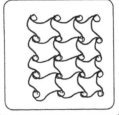

Tangles used: Cadent variation, N'Zeppel, Poke Root and Poke Leaf with Florz in the background.

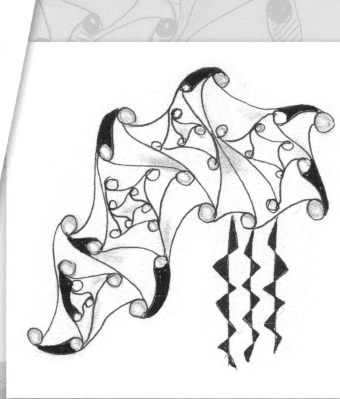

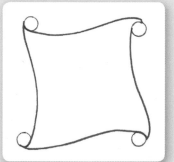

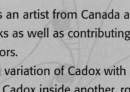

Cadox

(By Margaret Bremner CZT, Canada)
http://enthusiasticartist.blogspot.co.uk

Margaret is an artist from Canada and has written many books as well as contributing to books by other authors.

This is a variation of Cadox with one 'square' of Cadox inside another, rotating each time as in the diagram – how many you can add depends on the size of the first one. You can then do variations of Cadox as shown in the illustrations.

Tangles used:
Cadox and Rain

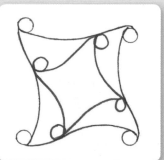

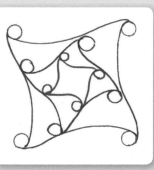

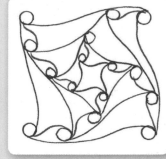

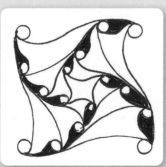

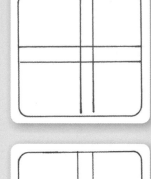

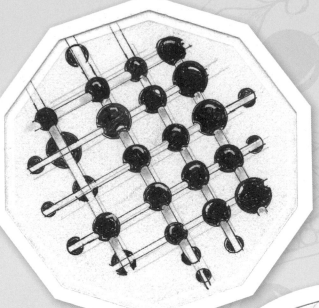

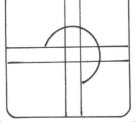

Tangles used:
Chemystery, Hollibaugh,
Luv-a and Tipple.

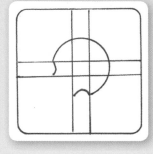

Chemystery
(By MaryAnn Scheblein-Dawson CZT, USA)

This tangle looks a little complicated when you see it completed, but it really is very simple and fun to do. I used a circle template for uniformity but you can do it freehand for a different effect. Leave a little crescent shape blank for a highlight, or use a white Gelly Roll pen as I have done on some of these orbs.

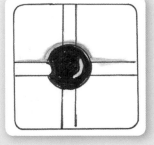

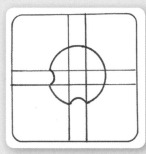

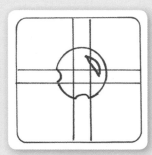

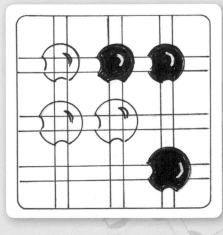

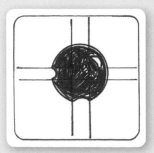

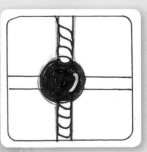

Copada
(By Margaret Bremner CZT, Canada)
http://enthusiasticartist.blogspot.co.uk

Copada is a really pretty pattern and not difficult to do. It makes an attractive border, whether it is straight or curved as in the illustration. Here I made a Zendala with Copada around the outside and a grid pattern in the middle, a zigzag running through the squares and alternating vertical and horizontal lines. I added a little colour for effect.

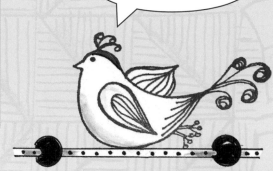

Don't worry if you can't think what to do next; leave it and come back later

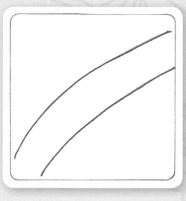

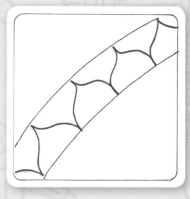

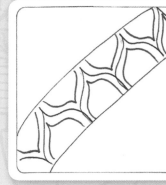

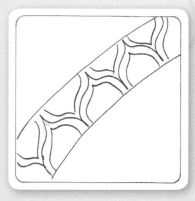

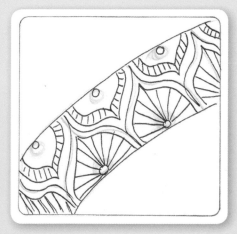

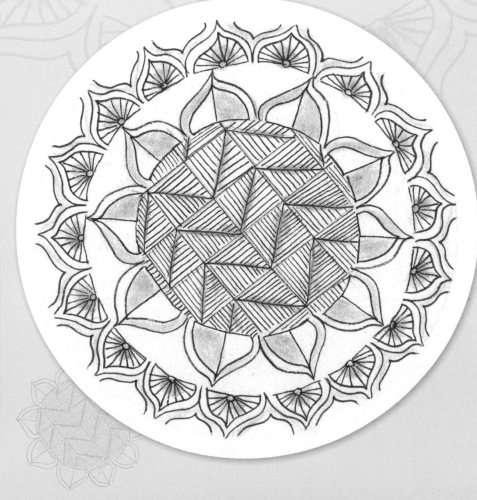

Cruffle

(By Sandy Hunter CZT, USA)
http://tanglebucket.blogspot.co.uk

Cruffle is one of my favourite tangles as it is very easy to do and so effective. I sometimes use a protractor with circular apertures in it to achieve a uniform look. It's a tangle that I find good for decorating cards – see p.56, where it appears in the corner of the 105 card. Check out Sandy's blogspot for lots more ideas for Cruffle.

Tangles used:
Cruffle, Flux, Shattuck
variation and Tipple.

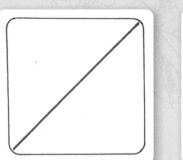

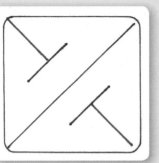

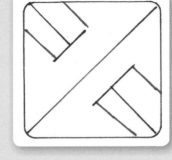

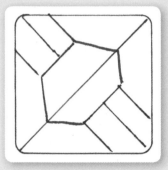

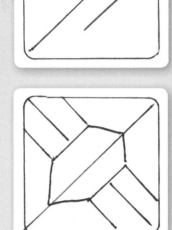

Crusade
(By Wayne Harlow CZT, USA)

I really enjoyed tackling this one as Wayne had done the step-out and shown a bigger picture with many Crusade tangles, accompanied by a note saying that it would be a good weekend challenge to work out how it was done. It took me a while, but once I realized that it was a grid (which can be straight or wavy) and that the corners need to meet up with another corner, I soon got the hang of which way to turn the whole thing so that I could start by doing the diagonal line in the right place. So there is a little hint of how it is done! Shading has given it an interesting architectural quality.

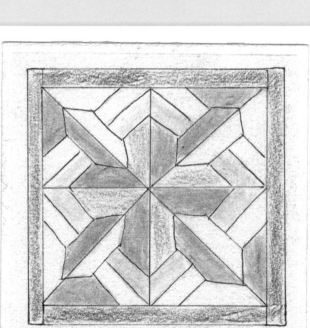

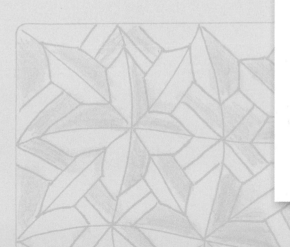

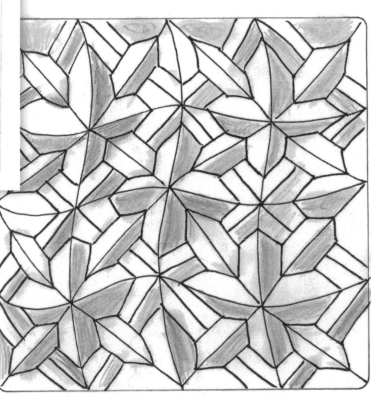

Cruze

(By Caren Mlot CZT, USA)
http://tanglemania.blogspot.co.uk

This is a fascinating tangle that needs a little practice to begin with but is well worth the effort as it looks very effective. Check out Caren's blogspot for more ideas on how to use it.

Tangles used:
Cruze and Luv-a.

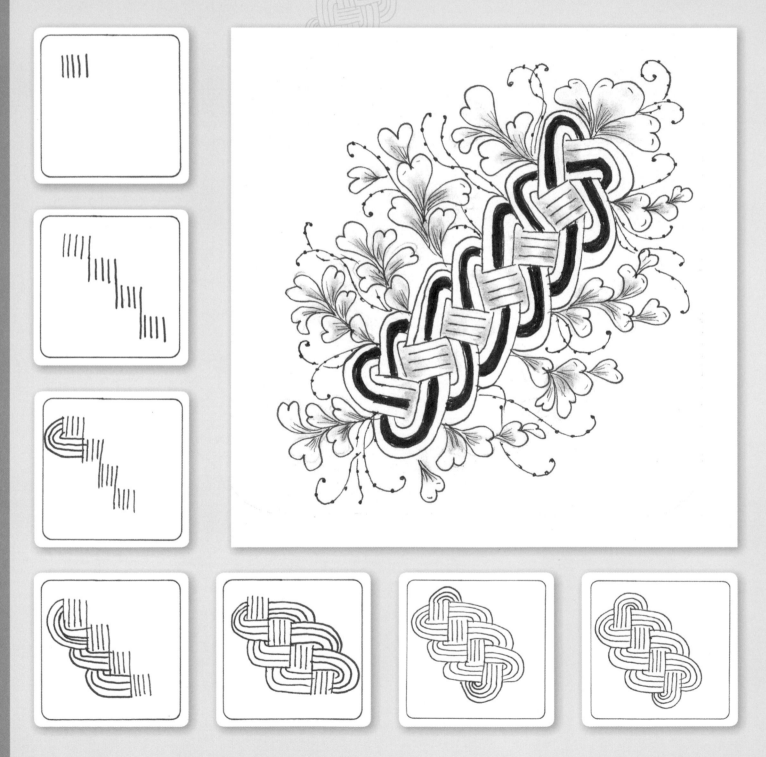

Curly Bracket Feather

(By Helen Williams CZT, Australia)
http://alittlelime.blogspot.co.uk

This is a lovely tangle by Helen which needs to be done quite carefully. Remembering that it's basically a bracket such as you would use in handwriting makes it easier – you may benefit from turning it in the direction that you would naturally draw a bracket. Go to Helen's blogspot for expert advice on drawing her tangles.

Here I have made a die-cut bookmark with a feather on it. I inked the edges with Distress Ink and coloured the feather with a Koh-i-Noor Magic Pencil. It is shown with a die-cut leaf on which I have done a simple pattern.

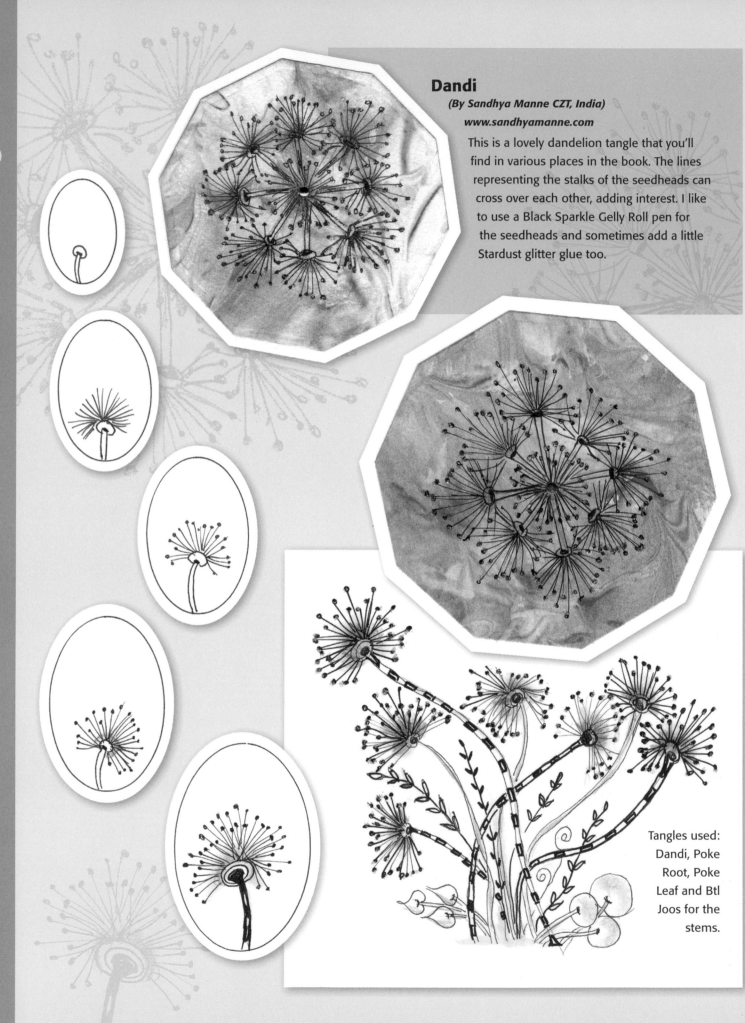

Dandi

(By Sandhya Manne CZT, India)

www.sandhyamanne.com

This is a lovely dandelion tangle that you'll find in various places in the book. The lines representing the stalks of the seedheads can cross over each other, adding interest. I like to use a Black Sparkle Gelly Roll pen for the seedheads and sometimes add a little Stardust glitter glue too.

Tangles used: Dandi, Poke Root, Poke Leaf and Btl Joos for the stems.

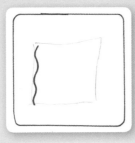

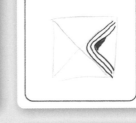

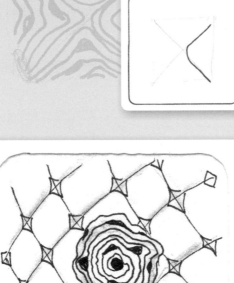

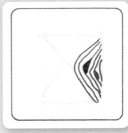

Tangles used: Divadance Rock 'n' Roll with Florz variation and Divadance Foxtrot with Mooka, both done on Bijou tiles.

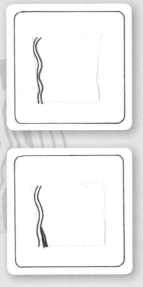

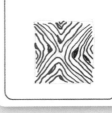

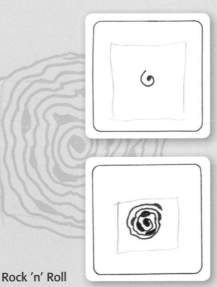

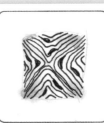

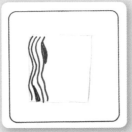

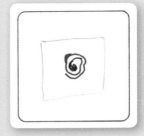

Divadance
(A Zentangle® original)

Divadance has three different styles: Waltz, Foxtrot and Rock 'n' Roll. I have stepped-out all three. It took me a few goes to get this tangle right when I first started to use it.

Foxtrot

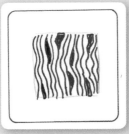

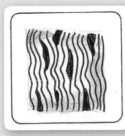

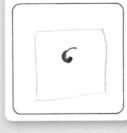

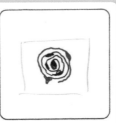

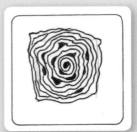

Waltz

Rock 'n' Roll

Turn the tile from time to time

Dragonair
(By Norma Burnell CZT, USA)

http://fairytangles.blogspot.co.uk

Dragonair is a very popular tangle and on Norma's blogspot you will find lots of ideas for it. In this illustration I put Dragonair around the outside with a Brax 'flower' in the middle with an aura around it. I added a little Puf Border as well.

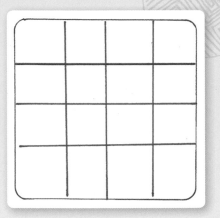

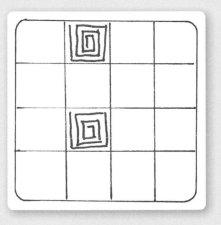

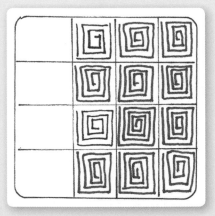

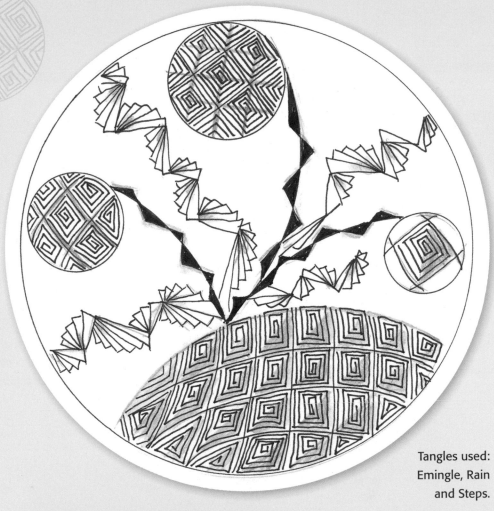

Tangles used:
Emingle, Rain
and Steps.

Emingle
(A Zentangle® original)

You can do this pattern as a uniform grid or make it uneven. It can be shaded in many ways, as shown below.

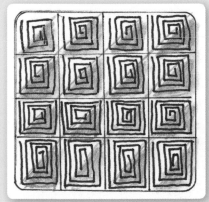

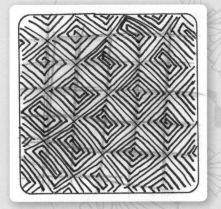

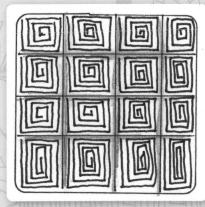

Fassett
(By Lynn Mead CZT, USA)

Lynn is an inspirational teacher who shares her ideas generously at Zentangle seminars. This is a really fascinating tangle with many variations.

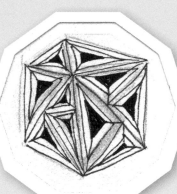

Tangles used: Fassett in the centre with Paradox around the edge and Widgets on a shaving foam background.

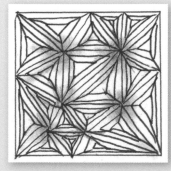

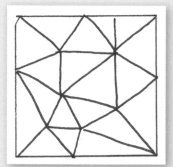

Draw triangles randomly.

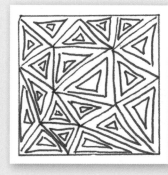

In each triangle, draw one or two more evenly spaced triangles.

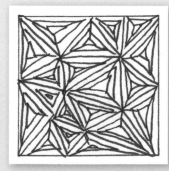

Starting at each corner of the smallest triangle, draw a line connecting the corners.

Add shading.

Fassett can be drawn with various grids, as shown in the diagrams. This adds to the versatility of Lynne's tangle.

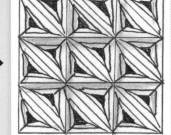
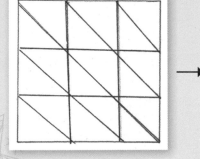

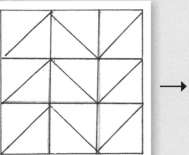
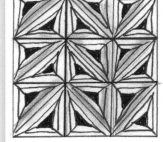

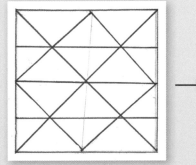
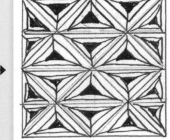

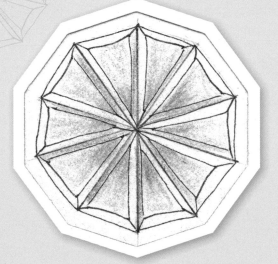

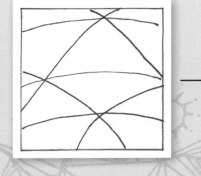
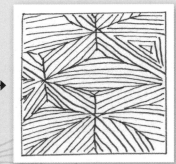

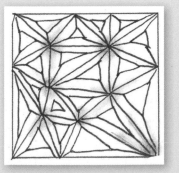

This variation uses one triangle only inside the outer triangle.

Feathers
(By Helen Williams CZT, Australia)
http://alittlelime.blogspot.co.uk

Helen is one of the most inspirational artists in the Zentangle world, and her e-books are full of beautiful artwork – *Light and Shadow* is particularly good if you want to explore the art of shading. Feathers is not difficult but needs a little care.

Tangles used:
Feathers and Mooka.

Fengle
(A Zentangle® original)

This tangle can be done in an even manner or with 'petals' of different sizes.

Tangles used: Fengle, Tipple and Cruffle with Flux.

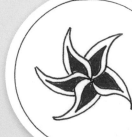

Heartline
(By Helen Williams CZT, Australia)
http://alittlelime.blogspot.co.uk
This is another great tangle from Helen and an easy one to do.

Tangles used:
Arukas, Crescent Moon, Flux, Heartline and Printemps.

Tangles used:
Btl Joos, Flux, Howda
and Marbaix.

Tangles used:
Btl Joos, N'Zeppel and
Steps with Howda
around the
edge.

Howda

(By Jane Marbaix CZT, UK)

www.zentanglewithjane.me

In the summer of 2014 I attended a get-together of European CZTs in Gouda in the Netherlands. The Dutch 'G' is pronounced rather like an 'H', hence the name of this tangle inspired by the patterns on the curtains in my room there. It gives you scope for creating lots of patterns by adding on to the base pattern – just keeping adding on to see where it takes you.

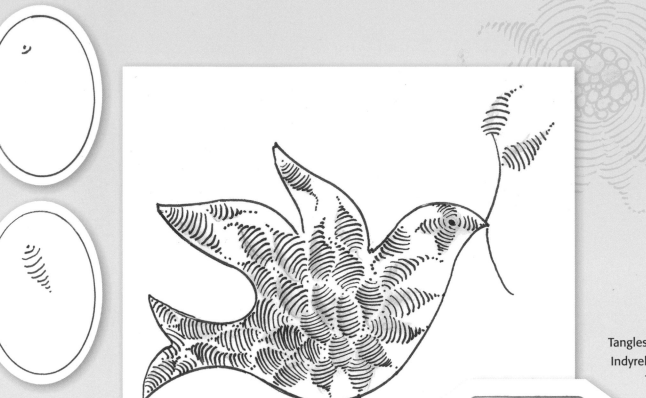

Tangles used:
Indyrella and
Tipple.

Indyrella
(A Zentangle® original)

This is another of Molly Hollibaugh's tangles. Practice is the key to this one as it's not quite as easy as it looks – you need to make sure there's a slight gap between each individual section. Adding some extra curve to it looks good. Here I've used it in the Dove stencil by Dreamweaver and on a die-cut decagon with the background coloured using the shaving foam method (see p.49).

Ixorus
(A Zentangle® original)

Draw the bands first, then if you keep rotating each time you add the half circles, putting one underneath the band and one on top all the way round, you will get the hang of it. Ixorus is a bit like Crescent Moon as you keep adding halos to the moon shapes.

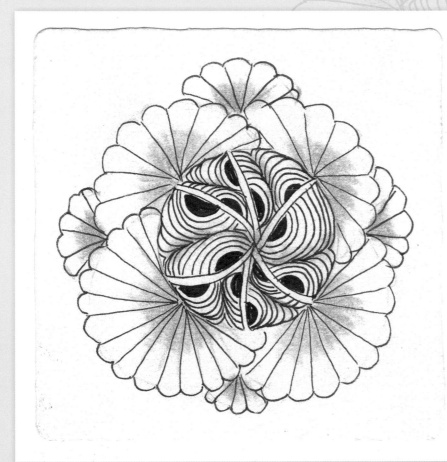

Tangles used:
Ixorus and Sanibelle.

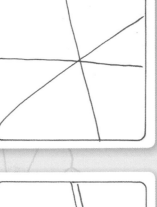

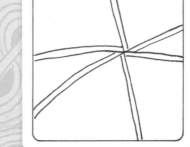

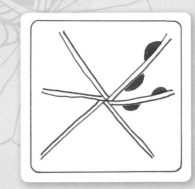

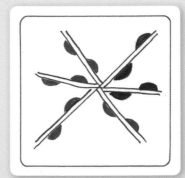

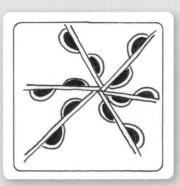

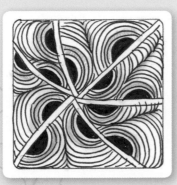

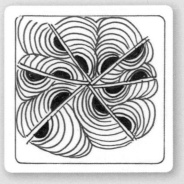

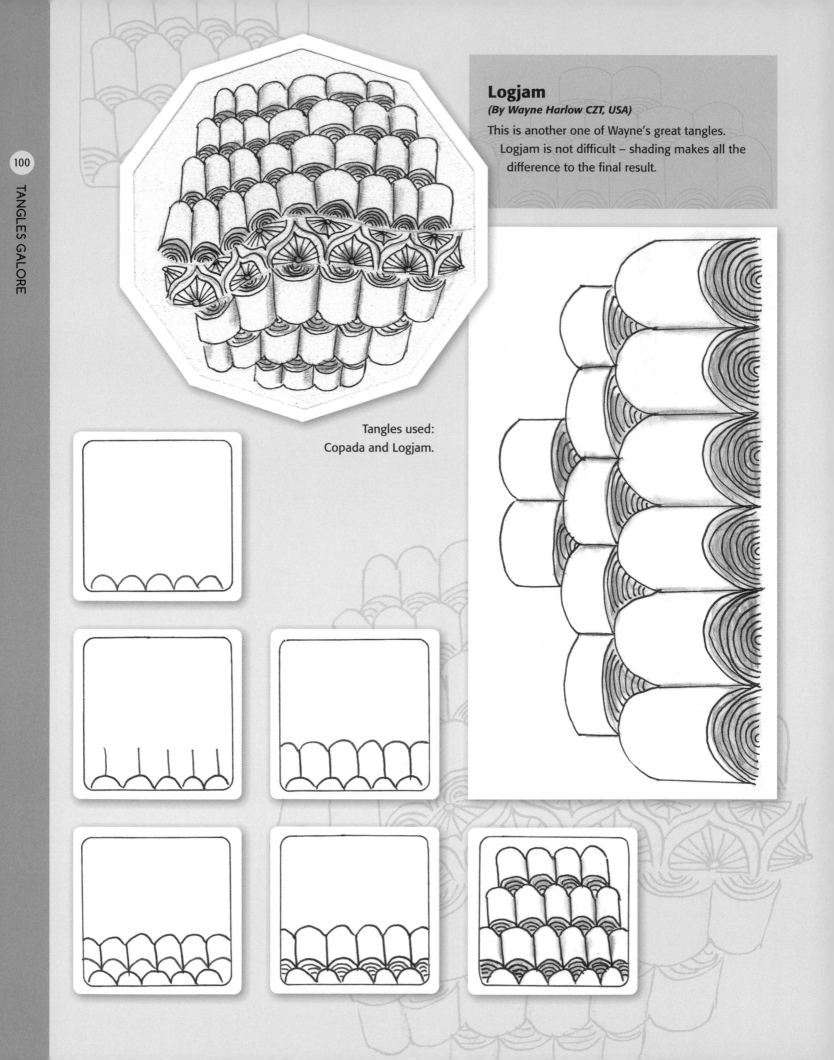

Logjam
(By Wayne Harlow CZT, USA)

This is another one of Wayne's great tangles. Logjam is not difficult – shading makes all the difference to the final result.

Tangles used:
Copada and Logjam.

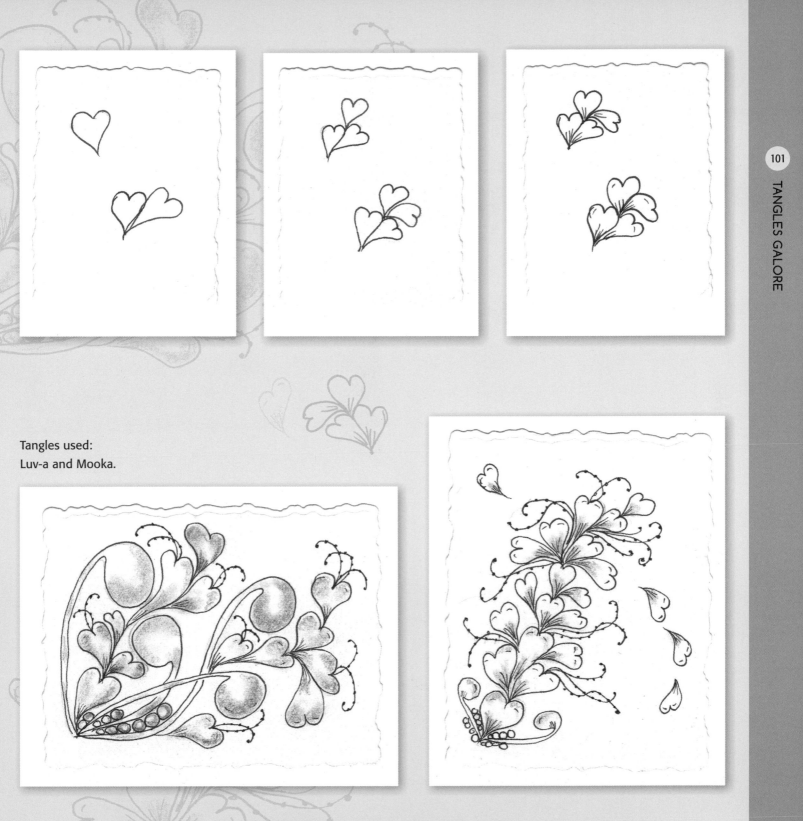

Tangles used:
Luv-a and Mooka.

Luv-a
(By Sharon Caforio CZT, USA)
This is such a pretty tangle to add to your Zentangle creations.
Take the hearts in as many directions as you like.

Tangles used: Dandi,
Mak-Rah-Meh, Poke
Root, Zinger, Widget and
Keeko (tree trunk).

Mak-Rah-Meh

(By Michelle Beauchamp CZT, Australia)
http://shellybeauch.blogspot.co.uk

If you have ever done macramé you will recognize this
very clever tangle as just like the basic knot.

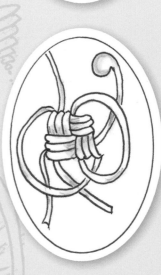

Marbaix

(By Jane Marbaix CZT, UK)

www.zentanglewithjane.me

This was my first tangle creation, inspired by an envelope I received. Here I have used a Dreamweaver vase stencil.

Tangles used:
Brax, Marbaix and Trumpits.

Maryhill

(By Betsy Wilson CZT, Canada)
http://craftsbybetsy.blogspot.co.uk

This is a really fascinating tangle which magically transforms into a windmill. It is fun to play around with and would make an attractive centre for a Zendala. In the larger mandala Maryhill is used with Paradox in every other triangle – it is quite similar and blends in well.

Remember to breathe

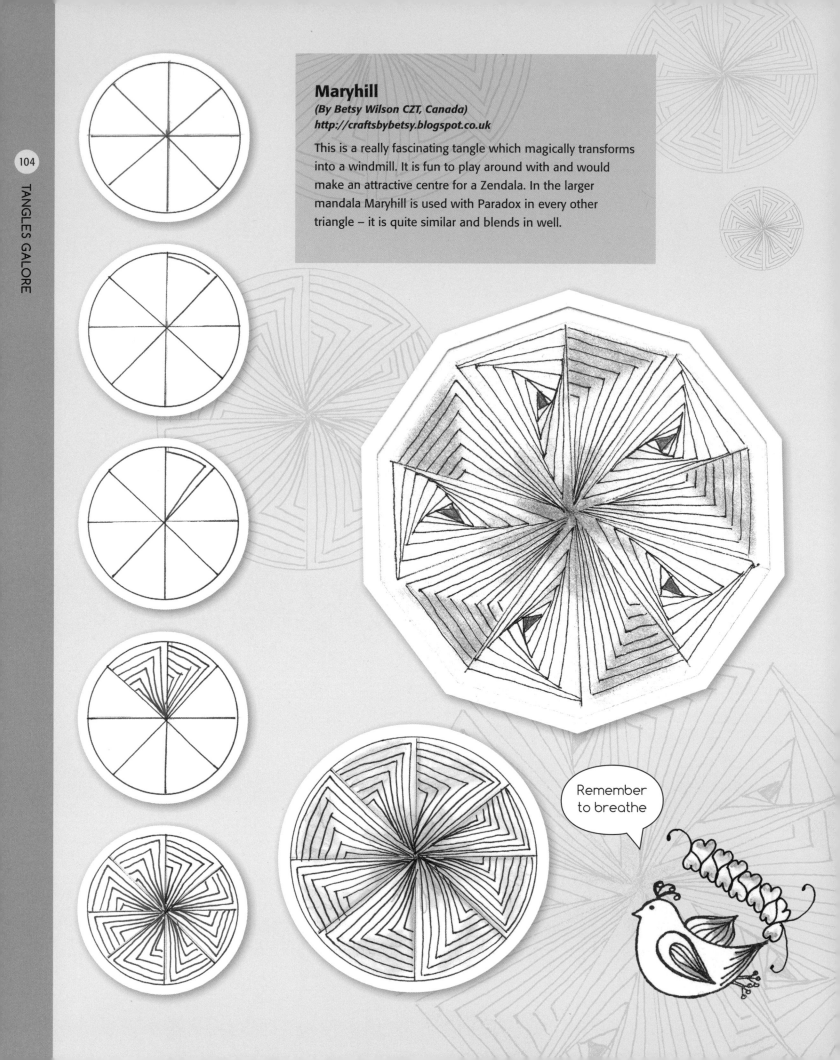

Matuvu

(By Rita Nikolajeva CZT, Latvia)

This is a very clever tangle, deconstructed into an easy step-out to follow. It looks a bit like knitting or knots. Vary the look by making the bottom or top loops bigger.

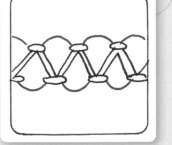

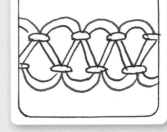

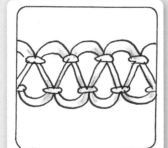

Tangles used: Matuvu and Showgirl.

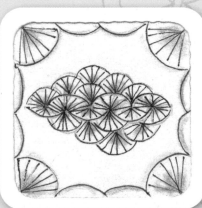

Tangles used: Matuvu and Fans.

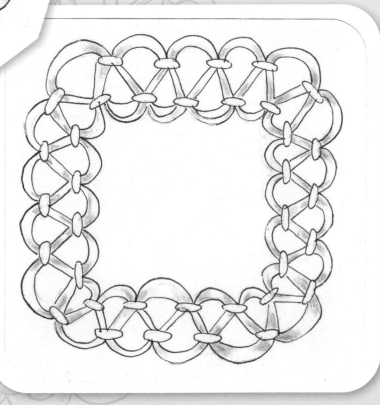

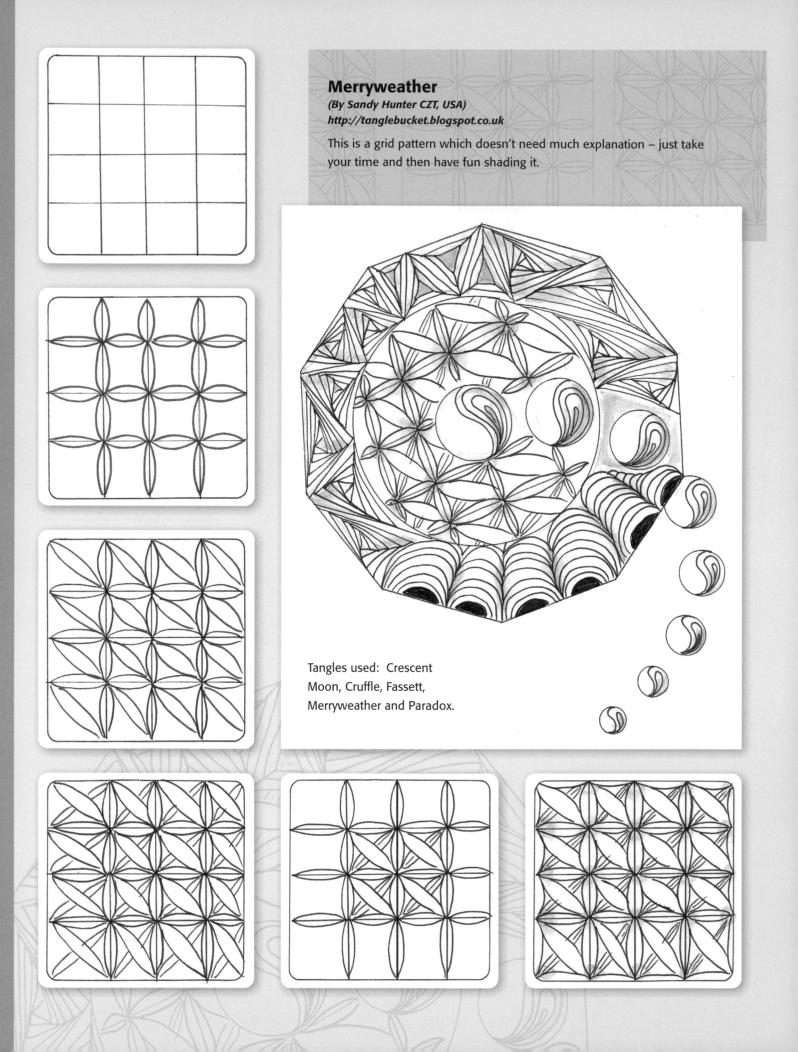

Merryweather

(By Sandy Hunter CZT, USA)
http://tanglebucket.blogspot.co.uk

This is a grid pattern which doesn't need much explanation – just take your time and then have fun shading it.

Tangles used: Crescent Moon, Cruffle, Fassett, Merryweather and Paradox.

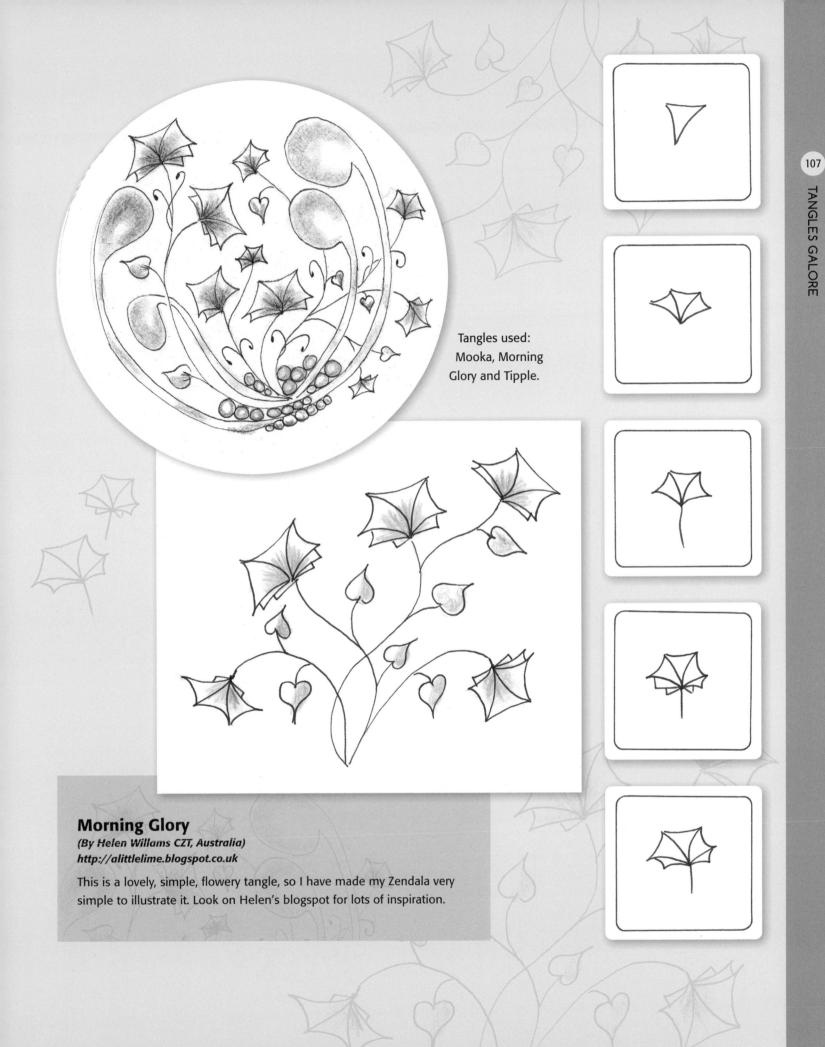

Tangles used:
Mooka, Morning
Glory and Tipple.

Morning Glory
(By Helen Willams CZT, Australia)
http://alittlelime.blogspot.co.uk

This is a lovely, simple, flowery tangle, so I have made my Zendala very
simple to illustrate it. Look on Helen's blogspot for lots of inspiration.

N'Zeppel
(A Zentangle® original)

This tangle is one that I use all the time. I have done the step-out using a uniform grid, but there is a random version where you draw a non-uniform string and then fill in with the squashed orbs like this one. One of my friends remarked that she loved my genie lamp stencil, so I have used it as a lamp in this Zendala – but if you rotate it you will see that it is actually a fish!

Tangles used:
Copada, Crescent
Moon, Knightsbridge
and N'Zeppel.

Tangles used: Onion Drops, Flux, Mooka and Tipple.

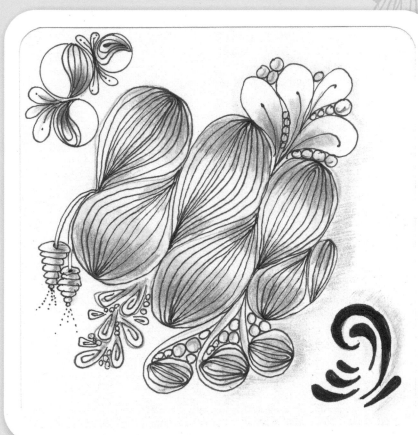

Onion Drops
(By Shasta Garcia, USA)

This tangle is fun to do and not complicated, though the lines need to touch the top of the initial shape for the right effect. After a while the first outline flows well. Adding colour makes this tangle even more attractive.

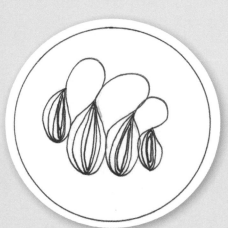

Tangles used, clockwise from top:
Borbz, Mooka, Auraknot, Brax,
Fassett, Arukas, Angel Fish,
Auraleah, Copada
and Bookee.

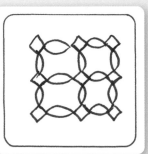

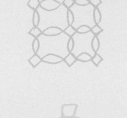

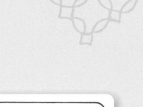

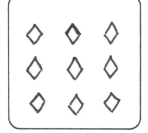

Oof

(A Zentangle® original)

This tangle by Rick and Maria is fairly simple. It lends itself to variation by adding something extra within the circles, as in the small illustration, or by blacking out some of the diamonds as I have done in the centre of my Zendala.

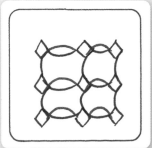

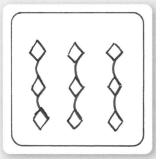

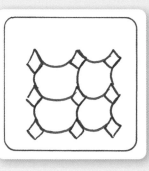

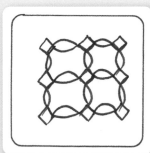

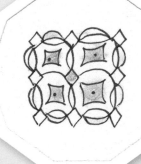

Oolo

(By Amelie Liao CZT)

There are CZTs all over the world, including China, Japan and the far east. I have coloured my artwork here with a Koh-i-Noor Magic Pencil.

Tangles used on Jelly Fish stencil by Dreamweaver: Oolo, Btl Joos, Crescent Moon and Meer.

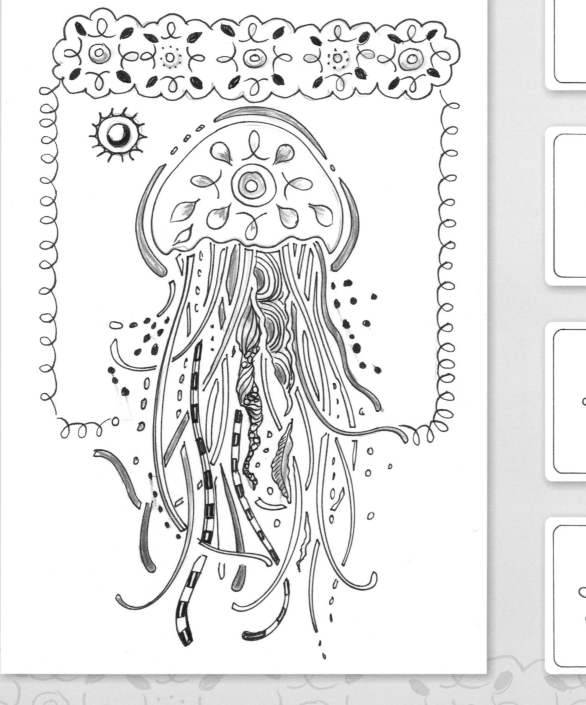

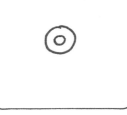

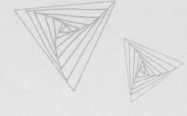

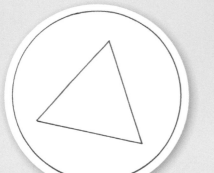

Paradox
(A Zentangle® original)

This is known as Rick's Paradox because Rick Roberts created it. I have done my artwork on a Zentangle Renaissance tile (available from www.zentangle. com), using brown and sepia pens as well and shading it with a white charcoal pencil. On the small die-cut shape I have done Paradox in a square for a different effect.

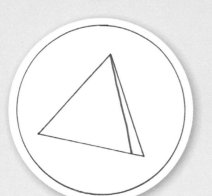

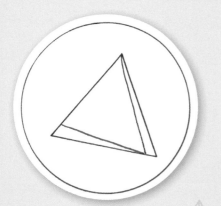

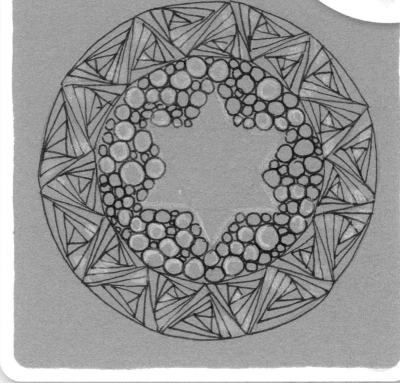

Tangles used: Paradox and Tipple.

Pendrils
(A Zentangle® original)

This is a bit like a series of knots. Maria does wonders with it, so it is worth looking it up on www.tanglepatterns.com.

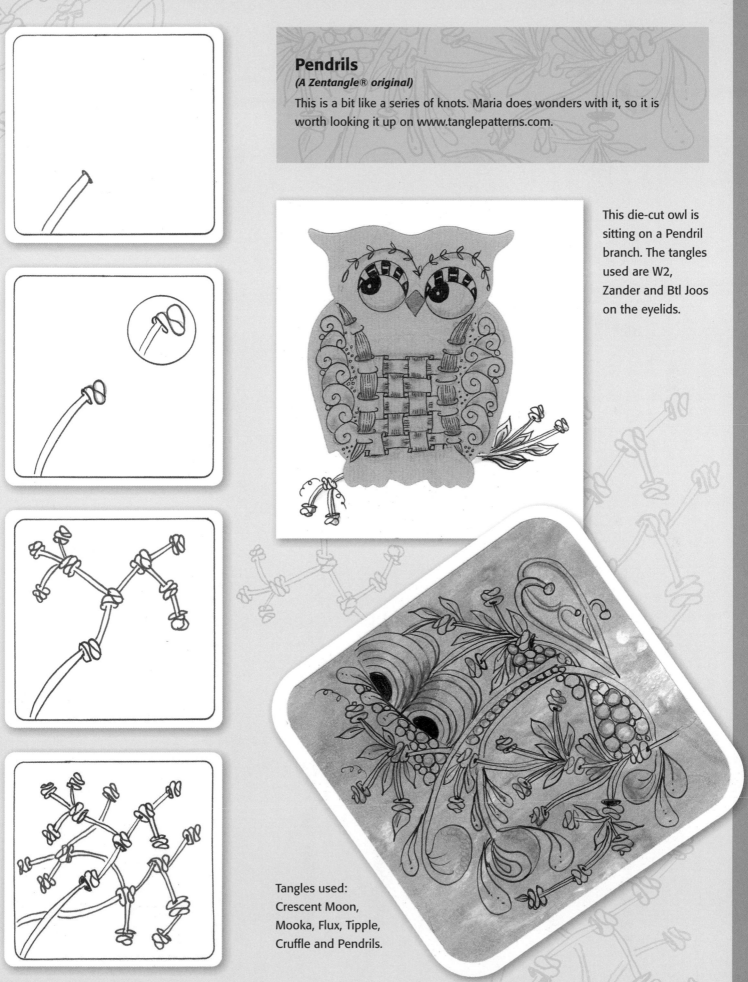

This die-cut owl is sitting on a Pendril branch. The tangles used are W2, Zander and Btl Joos on the eyelids.

Tangles used: Crescent Moon, Mooka, Flux, Tipple, Cruffle and Pendrils.

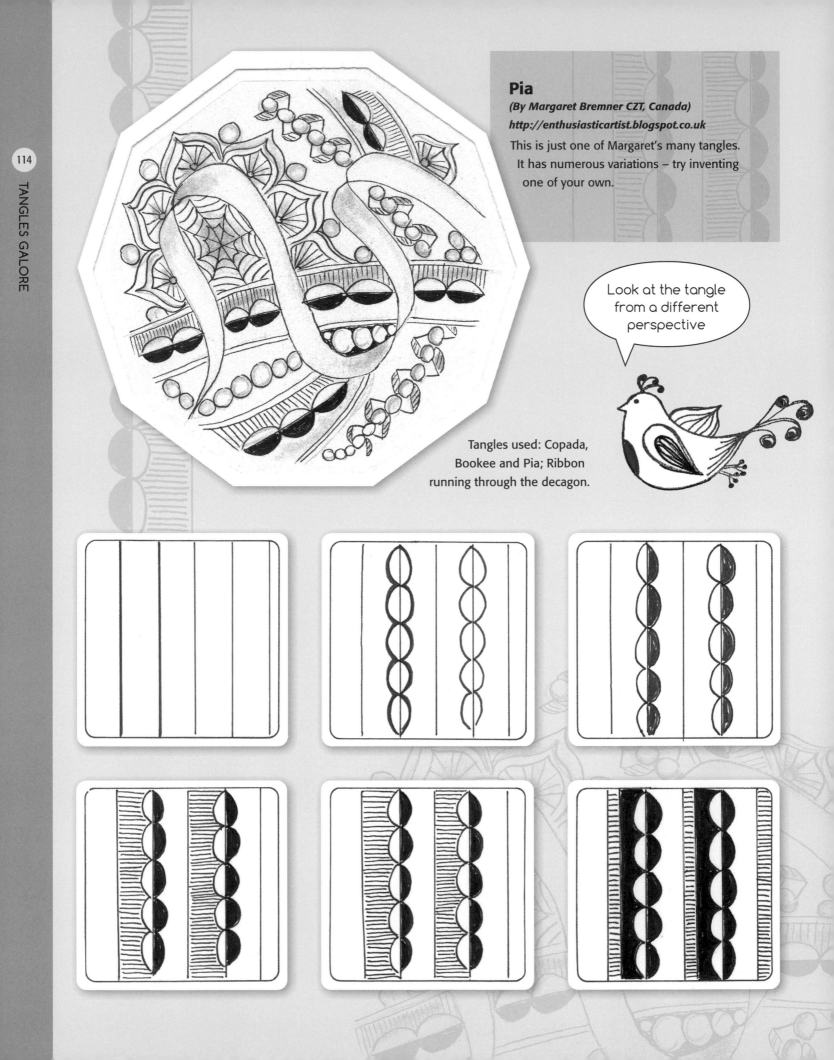

Pia
(By Margaret Bremner CZT, Canada)
http://enthusiasticartist.blogspot.co.uk

This is just one of Margaret's many tangles. It has numerous variations – try inventing one of your own.

Look at the tangle from a different perspective

Tangles used: Copada, Bookee and Pia; Ribbon running through the decagon.

POMX2
(By Mei Hua Teng [AKA Damy])

Damy's pretty grid-pattern tangle is easy to replicate. You can vary the look by changing the size of the diamond shape.

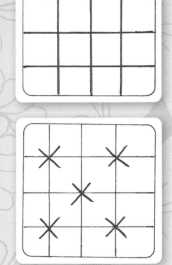

Tangles used: POMX2 in the centre with Pia around the outside.

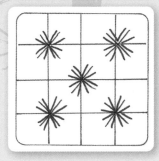

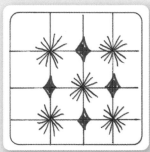

Tangles used: Showgirl is in the centre with a circle of leaves and on the outer circle is POMX2.

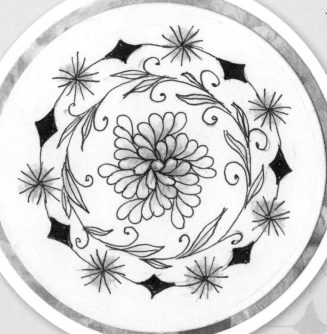

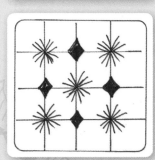

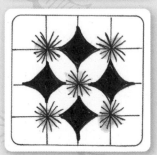

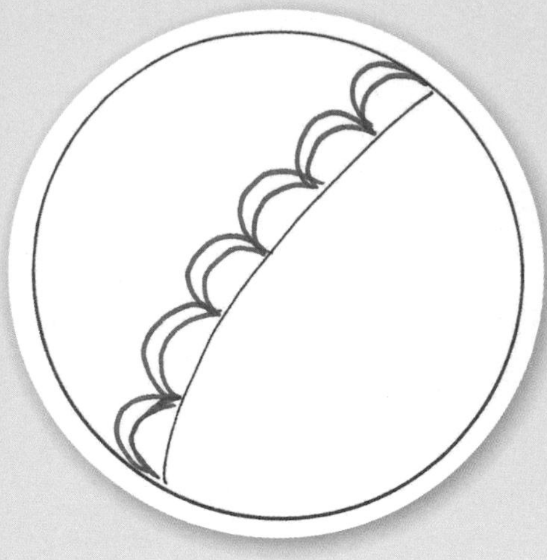

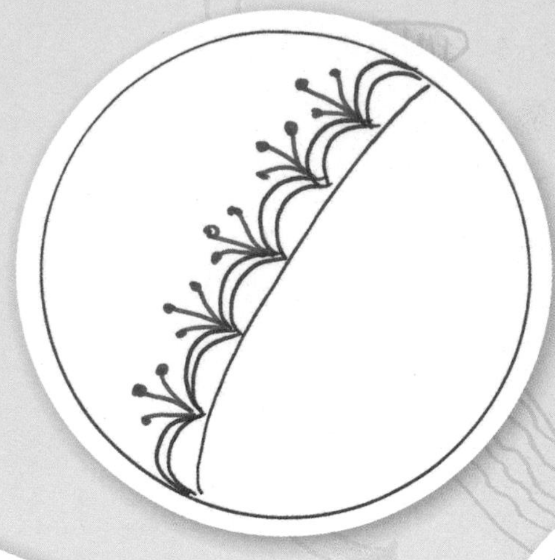

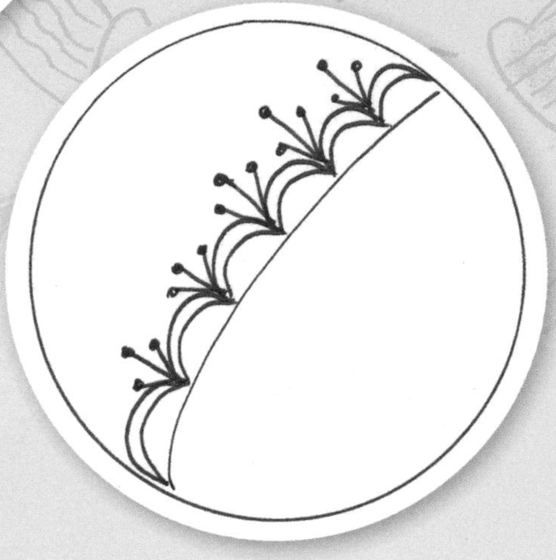

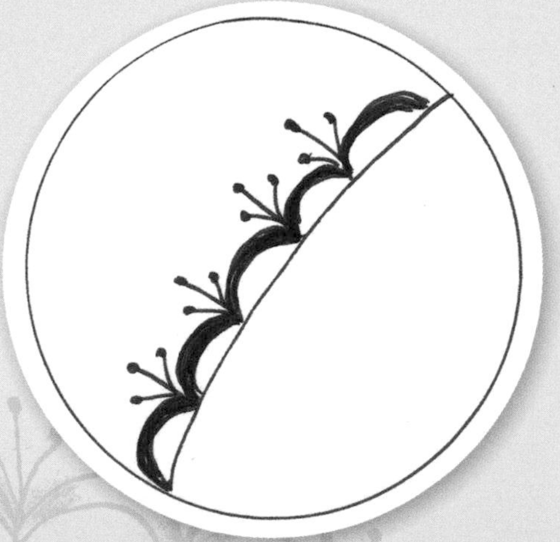

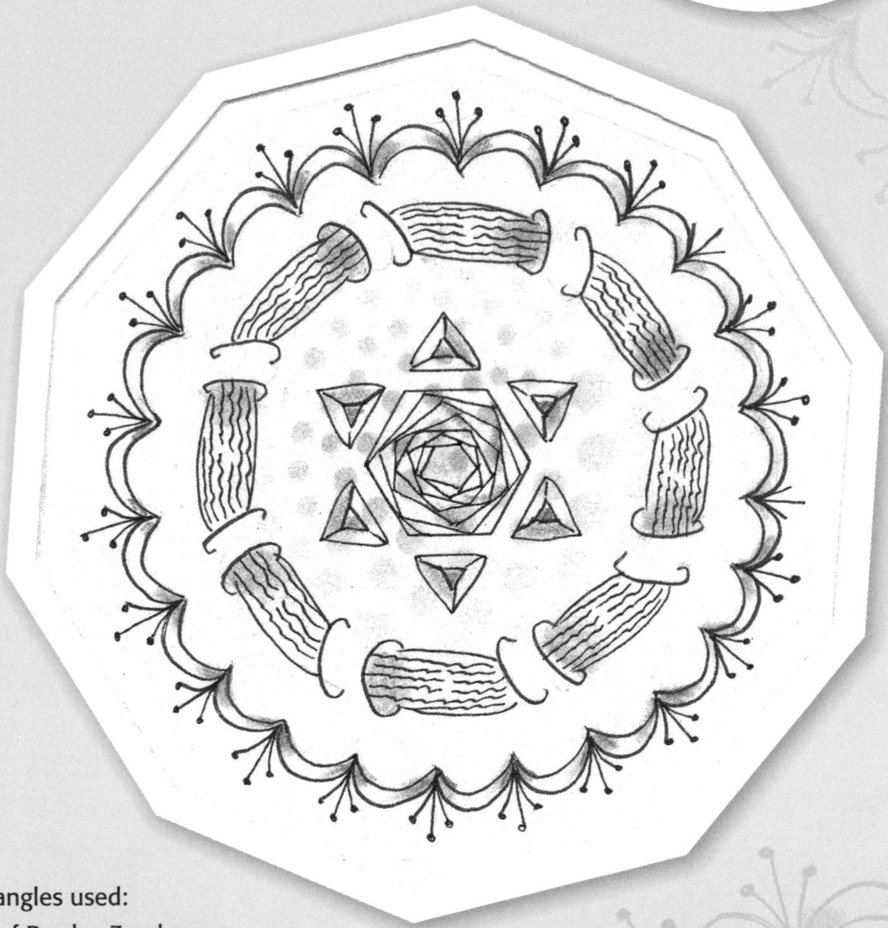

Tangles used:
Puf Border, Zander,
Fassett and Paradox

Puf Border
(By Suzanne McNeil CZT, USA)

This really is a lively tangle, and June Bailey has used it on her
seahorse Zendala to great effect (see p.52).

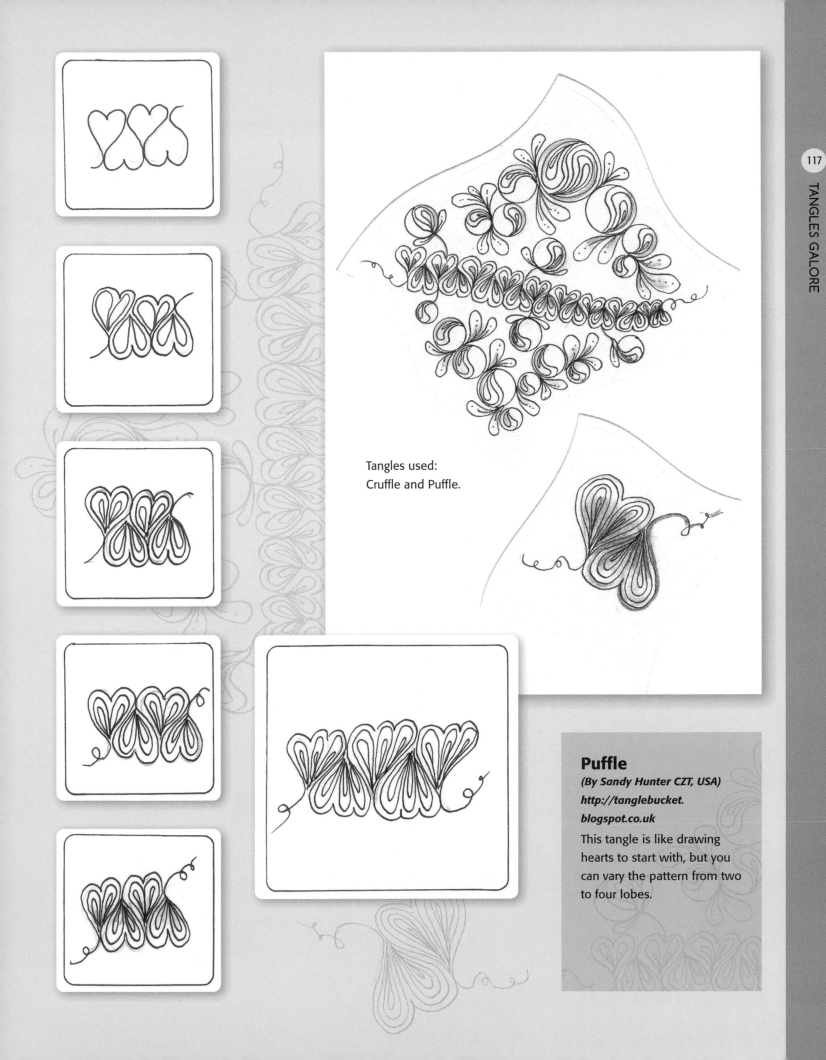

Tangles used:
Cruffle and Puffle.

Puffle

(By Sandy Hunter CZT, USA)
http://tanglebucket.
blogspot.co.uk

This tangle is like drawing
hearts to start with, but you
can vary the pattern from two
to four lobes.

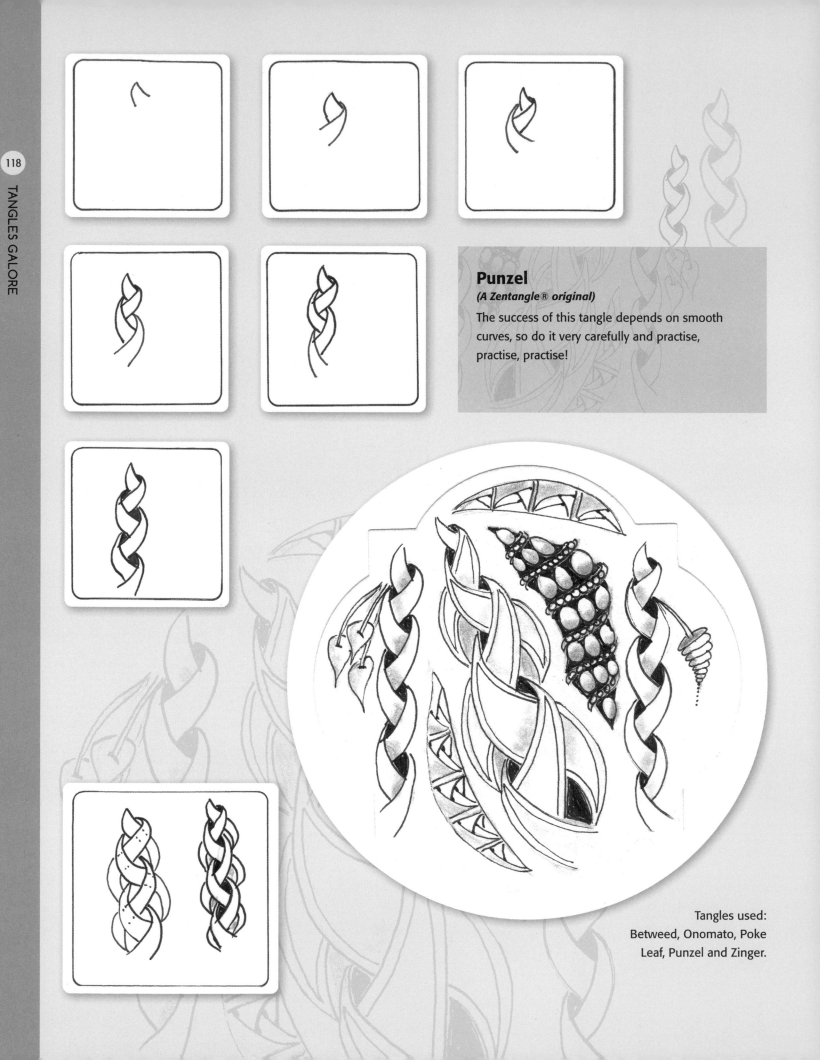

Punzel
(A Zentangle® original)

The success of this tangle depends on smooth curves, so do it very carefully and practise, practise, practise!

Tangles used:
Betweed, Onomato, Poke Leaf, Punzel and Zinger.

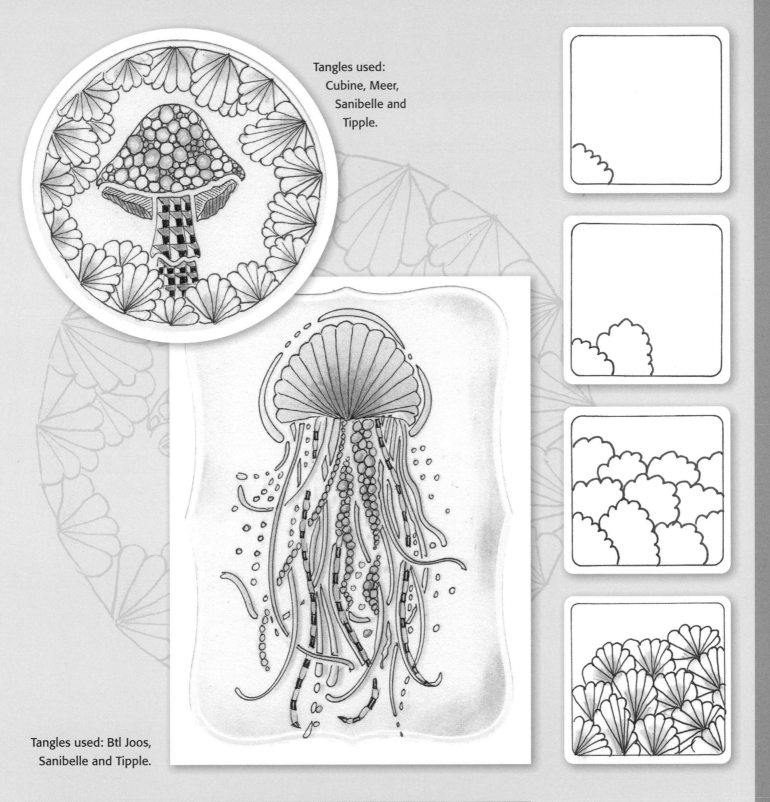

Tangles used:
Cubine, Meer,
Sanibelle and
Tipple.

Tangles used: Btl Joos,
Sanibelle and Tipple.

Sanibelle
(By Tricia Faraone CZT, USA)
http://tanglewithme-tricialee.blogspot.co.uk

Tricia comes from Rhode Island and the beautiful Sanibelle Beach inspired her to do this tangle. It is featured in June's seahorse Zendala on p.52 and I have used it here in Jelly Fish and Toadstool stencils by Dreamweaver.

Tangles used:
Cruffle, Joy, Marbaix
and Scrawlz.

Scrawlz

(By Jane Dickinson CZT, USA)

www.TheMindfulDrawer.com

Jane says: 'I have been a CZT since 2010. As with so many people, Zentangle entered my life at a very difficult time, exactly when I needed a haven of simplicity and calm. Meeting the founders, Rick Roberts and Maria Thomas, revealed why Zentangle is the accessible, unpretentious, lovely artform that it is. Zentangle continues to guide both my daily and life decisions and through it I have connected with some amazing people who have discovered the extraordinary in themselves.'

Jane's account explains what Zentangle means to so many people. I found Scrawlz to be such a pretty tangle to do and I love the simplicity of it. It would make a delightful border or embellishment on a greetings card.

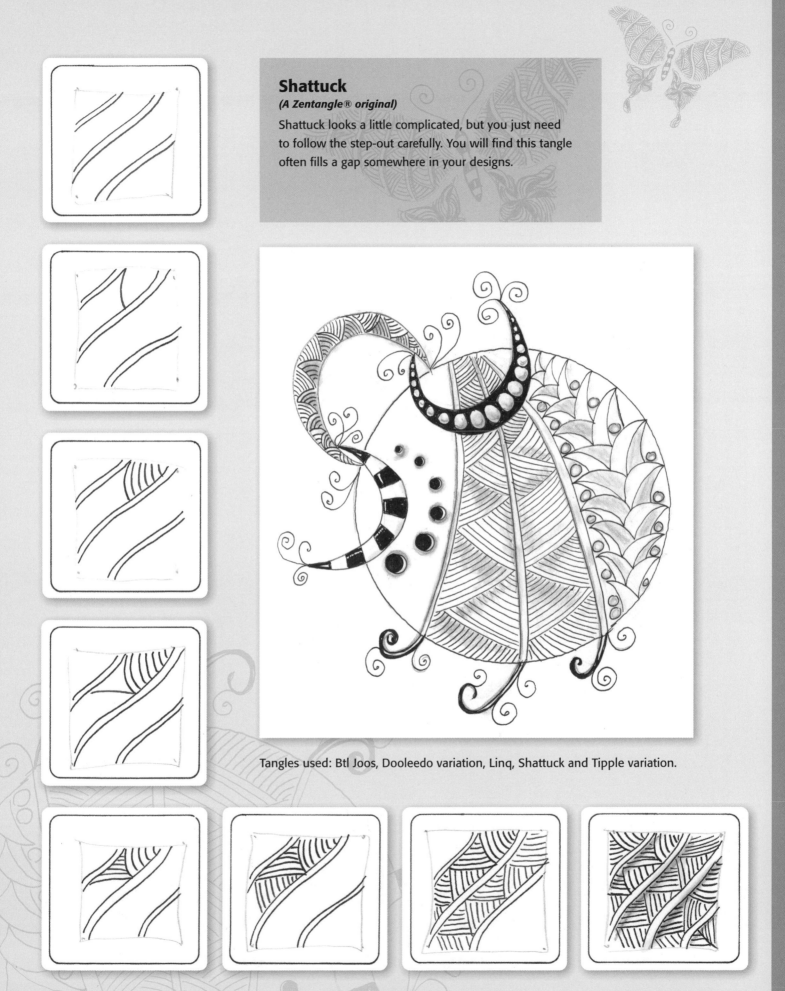

Shattuck
(A Zentangle® original)

Shattuck looks a little complicated, but you just need to follow the step-out carefully. You will find this tangle often fills a gap somewhere in your designs.

Tangles used: Btl Joos, Dooleedo variation, Linq, Shattuck and Tipple variation.

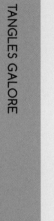
Showgirl
(By Vicki Bassett, USA)

This is a lovely flowery tangle, starting in the middle and working outwards.

Have a look at Rita Nikolajeva's Zendalas on pp.33–5 and you will see it done perfectly. Here I have used the seahorse stencil by Dreamweaver, adding a little colour and applying some Black Sparkle Gelly Roll pen on Showgirl.

Tangles used:
Crescent Moon
and Showgirl.

Tangles used:
Sparkle with a
touch of Fescu.

Sparkle

(By Sharon Caforio CZT, USA)

I feel there's a little bit of magic
along with the Sparkle tangle
by Sharon. It is simple to do but
effective. In my artwork I have used
some coloured pencils and a gem in
the middle. I achieved the effect by
starting with a cross in pencil.

Steps

(By Helen Williams CZT, Australia)
http://alittlelime.blogspot.co.uk

You can have lots of fun with this one and I have shown three different ways of doing it. The first is a straight line with straight lines added; the second is a curvy line with straight lines added and the third is a curvy line with curvy pattern added. Look at Helen's blog for lots of other ideas.

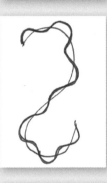

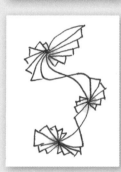

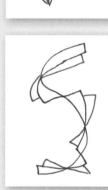

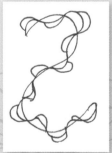

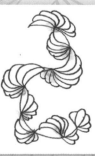

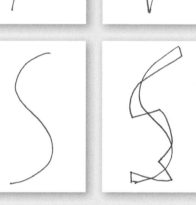

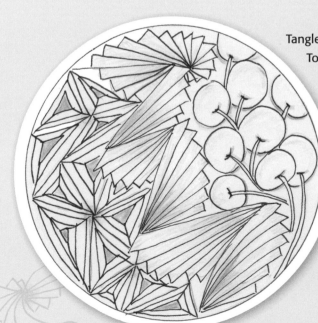

Tangles used:
Top: Steps and Mooka.
Left: Steps, Fassett and
Poke Root with some
colour added.

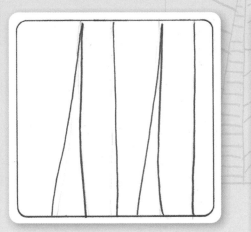

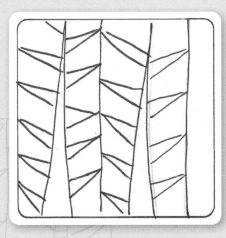

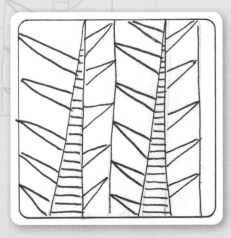

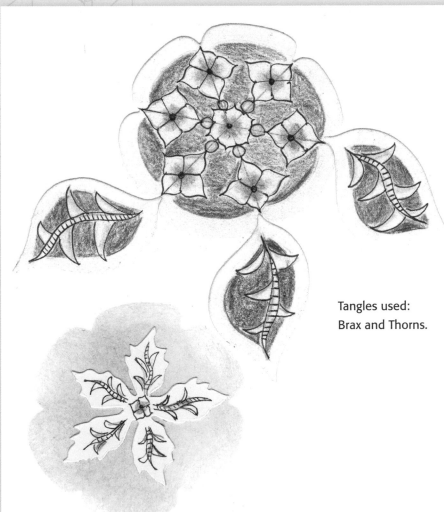

Tangles used:
Brax and Thorns.

Thorns
(By Suzanne McNeill CZT, USA) **www.blog.suzannemcneill.com**

This pattern is from Suzanne's book *Zentangle 7*, which has many inspiring designs. As you can see, the tangle can be drawn with straight or curvy stems.

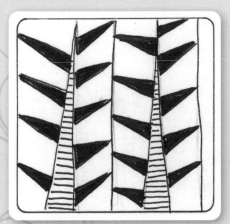

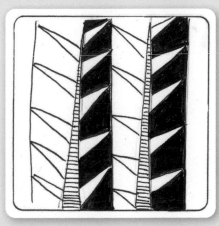

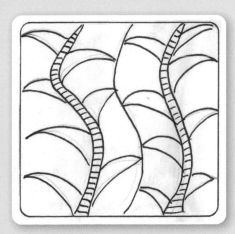

Tangles used:
Cruffle and
Whirlee.

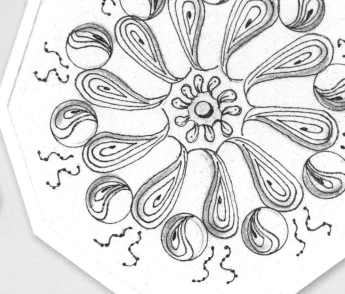

Whirlee
(By Lynn Mead CZT, USA)

Whirlee is named with the seedpods of the sycamore tree in mind. It is fun to play around with. The first Zendala is done by dividing the decagon in pencil from corner to corner and then doing Whirlee in a circle, all in the same direction.

Tangles used:
Whirlee back to back,
filled in with Flux and
Fassett in between.

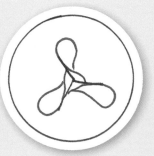

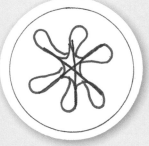

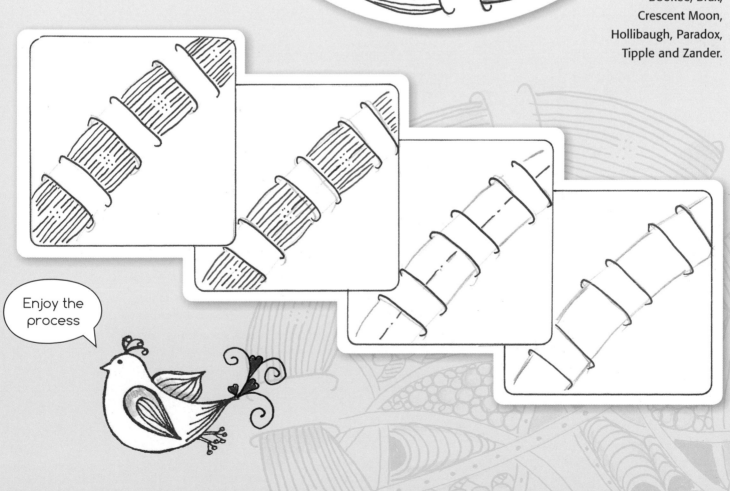

Zander
(A Zentangle® original)

I use Zander a lot, as it is a good tangle for running through a larger design. I like to curve the bottom and top lines to make it look as though the bands are tightened around the stem. I have left highlights in the middle to give a rounded effect and added shading on one side of the band. In the artwork, I drew the other tangles in the spaces created by Hollibaugh.

Tangles used:
Bookee, Brax,
Crescent Moon,
Hollibaugh, Paradox,
Tipple and Zander.

Enjoy the process

Calmness of mind
is one of the
beautiful jewels
of wisdom

Tangles used, clockwise from top left:
Morning Glory, Steps, Garlic Cloves
with Zingers, Fassett, Paradox,
Poke Root and Btl Joos.

There is so much to occupy us in the 21st century that it's easy to feel there isn't time to just switch off and be ourselves rather than worrying about what needs to be done next to maintain a job, a home or a family, or all three at once! But if you can set aside just a short time each day to create some stillness and calm by doing this magic that is Zentangle you will find that peace and relaxation will seep through into the rest of your life, transforming your days.